THE FATHER FACTOR

THE FATHER FACTOR

Peter O'Shea and Robert Falzon

Connor Court Publishing

Connor Court Publishing Pty Ltd

Copyright © Peter O'Shea & Robert Falzon 2014

ALL RIGHTS RESERVED. This book contains material protected under International and Federal Copyright Laws and Treaties. Any unauthorised reprint or use of this material is prohibited. No part of this book may be reproduced or transmitted in any form or by any means, electronic or mechanical, including photocopying, recording, or by any information storage and retrieval system without express written permission from the publisher.

PO Box 224W
Ballarat VIC 3350
sales@connorcourt.com
www.connorcourt.com

ISBN: 9781925138337 (pbk.)

Cover design by Ian James and Brent Lammas

Printed in Australia

*This book is dedicated to the loving memory
of our fathers,
Kevin O'Shea and John Falzon*

Table of Contents

1 Introduction	**1**
1.1 Book outline	7
2 The father factor	**8**
2.1 Fatherhood – the good and the bad	9
2.2 Demographic trends	11
2.3 The good news	14
2.4 Summary	16
3 The key drivers of success and happiness	**17**
3.1 Happiness and success	18
3.2 Related studies	24
3.3 Healthy physical ageing	26
3.4 Summary	28
4 The role of fathers	**29**
4.1 The quality of fatherly involvement	33
4.2 Fostering the development of children's potential	34
4.3 Nurturing the cognitive development of children	40
4.4 Nurturing the emotional and social development of children	43
4.5 Nurturing the physical health of children	45
4.6 Nurturing the moral and spiritual development of children	46
4.7 Providing nurture during adolescence	49
4.8 The other key roles of a father	50
4.9 Summary	50

5 Poor fathering and poor responses to fathering — 52
- 5.1 Poor fathering — 52
- 5.2 Poor responses to fathering — 59
- 5.3 Correcting poor behaviour — 62
- 5.4 Summary — 65

6 Turning the hearts of sons and daughters to parents — 67
- 6.1 The potential for restoration — 67
- 6.2 Starting the journey of restoration and healing – identifying the root causes — 70
- 6.3 The journey of behavioural change and restoration — 73
- 6.4 A Twelve Step approach to restoration — 74
- 6.5 Adjustment of beliefs and thinking processes — 83
- 6.6 Summary — 87

7 Turning the hearts of parents to sons and daughters — 89
- 7.1 Parental initiative — 89
- 7.2 Relationships and trauma — 92
- 7.3 The process of restoration — 95
- 7.4 The benefits of parental initiative for parents — 97
- 7.5 Summary — 99

8 Turning the hearts of fathers to mothers and mothers to fathers — 101
- 8.1 The co-parenting environment — 102
- 8.2 Summary — 105

9 Examining the evidence for the impact of spirituality on restoration — 106

9.1	The association between spirituality, happiness and mental health	106
9.2	The impact of spirituality on prevention and treatment of substance abuse	108
9.3	The mechanisms of restoration	112
9.4	Empathic capacity	122
9.5	Turning lemons into lemonade	125
9.6	Summary	128

10 Conclusions — **129**

   10.1 Where to from here? — 130

References — **133**

Appendix I: Personal stories — **147**
   Rough Diamond — 147
   Voyage without my father — 156
   A wife and mother's perspective — 163

Appendix II: Supporting evidence — **165**
   AII.1 Examining the evidence for the effectiveness of Alcoholics Anonymous — 165
   AII.2 Risk rates for youth incarceration as a function of family type — 172
   AII.3 Influence of parents on children's spiritual engagement — 173

Appendix III: A selection of resources — **174**

Index — **178**

Abbreviations

AA	Alcoholics Anonymous
AC	Alternating Current
TB	Tuberculosis
IQ	Intelligence Quotient
NB	Nucleus Basalis
PORN	Pornography
CBT	Cognitive Behaviour Therapy
VA	Veterans' Administration
RCT	Randomised Controlled Trial
OR	Odds Ratio
TV	Television

1

Introduction

For many people success and happiness are sadly elusive. No matter what they do, it seems, life does not work out for them. Sometimes when such people experience the frustration of ongoing failure and sadness they simply console themselves with the notion that 'life is not fair' – but is that really true? Is it possible, rather, that there might be some key forces operating to determine destinies, of which we might be unaware?

In trying to improve life circumstances, there are many who travail much but achieve little. Confronted by unmet expectations and unfulfilled dreams, some people might start trying to put in longer hours or save more diligently or apply for more jobs. These actions, good though they might be in themselves, are not the keys to unlocking a fulfilling and productive life. To find those keys it is necessary to look to the evidence.

Over many decades studies have been conducted to determine what it is that impacts most powerfully on success and happiness. Those studies have provided some compelling answers. Among the many factors which have been measured in empirical studies, four key factors have been found to influence success and happiness very strongly. They are the *father factor*, the *mother factor*, the *relationship (or love) factor* and the *addiction factor* (Allen and Daly, 2007; Erickson, 2011; McLanahan and Sandefur, 1997; Vaillant, 2002; Vaillant, 2012). These four factors are truly destiny shaping influences.

This book touches on all four of the above factors, but gives particular focus to the father factor. The reason for this focus is not that the father factor is the most important of the four – rather, it is that the father factor is in particularly great need of attention. Relatively few children grow up without their biological mother, but many children grow up without their biological father. About one third of American children currently live away from their biological father, and some estimates indicate that about half of them will live away from their father for at least part of their childhood (Solomon-Fears et al, 2013).

The father factor is also a gatekeeper for the other key factors. Humans imbibe foundational relationship skills during the early years of life when the father and mother have tremendous influence. For better or worse, fathers really do affect their children's relationships. The teen pregnancy rate in New Zealand and America, for example, has been found to be about seven to eight times lower in intact families than it is in families where the father is absent before his daughter reaches age five. The rate is about two to three times lower in intact families than it is in families where father absence sets in between ages 6-13. (Ellis et al, 2003).

The father factor also impacts on the addiction factor. A Swedish study found that girls from single parent families were more than three times as likely to die from an addiction to drugs or alcohol as girls from two parent families. Swedish boys from single parent families were found to be about five times as likely to die from an addiction to drugs or alcohol as those in two parent families (Weitoft et al, 2003).

The father factor even affects the mother factor. An involved and loving father shares the parenting duties. This kind of responsible sharing helps the mother to be a more effective parent (Amato, 1998; Biller, 1993).

CASE STUDY: My (Robert's) parents raised their children in a difficult environment and economy. They were/are good people. They were well intentioned and tried hard, but with five children to feed, clothe, school and care for, there was never much money. There also never seemed to be much time for quality relationships.

Like many other families of the time, Mum served in the home and carried out most of the child raising duties except the disciplining. Dad was the boss, provided the discipline (sometimes harsh and physical), and worked two jobs in the early part of my life just to provide and put food on the table and pay the bills. Sadly, in our family there always seemed to be too many bills and too little money.

My memory and experience of those times was that Dad was rarely home as a consequence of working two jobs and when he was at home he was exhausted and emotionally absent. We did not have a close relationship in those childhood years. I thought he loved me and I loved him, but we didn't do many things together. We didn't play much, he was not at the special events or present at my sporting activities and achievements.

The lack of a strong father-son relationship left me with many unanswered questions, confusion about who I was and what it was to be a man. My reflection is that I was searching and longing for affirmation, validation, modelling and instruction. It didn't come and I was left incomplete and strangely ashamed.

Now, I do not blame my father for any of this. It was not his fault. He did the best he could, given the times and the circumstances. His own upbringing left him significantly impaired and unfinished as a man. His father (my grandfather), Joseph, was a cook in the merchant navy. It was the era of steam driven vessels and long voyages across oceans and seas. Joseph was away most of Dad's life, coming home only for a few weeks a year. My recollection of my grandfather, Joseph, was a one off meeting. He was sitting at the laminex table in the small kitchen of his very part-time home, rolling his own cigarettes for that evening. I cannot remember what he said, if anything. I don't recall my Dad saying anything either. The only thing communicated was distance.

I think of these times with sadness and lost opportunities. My Dad and I were strangers. I knew almost nothing about him, what he felt, how he thought, what made him happy or sad. Did he have dreams and hopes? I wanted and needed so much from him. He held and contained something for me (and I for him) that no one else had or probably could give.

Life, grace and circumstances provided new opportunities for real relationship in Dad's later years. I was in my late thirties/early forties when we both intentionally sought each other out, became reconciled and built a warm and meaningful relationship. He made efforts to reveal his heart and mind. I made efforts to listen, learn and love.

Eventually, he said the words that I needed to hear — *"I love you Robbie." "I am so proud of you my son." "You have what it takes to be a great man."* Necessary, irreplaceable, delicious words that became flesh, which became a man ... me. We enjoyed each other, did things together, grew in relationship, laughed and cried, and as a consequence I grew as a man and he grew as a Dad. At this emotional banquet there was much healing, nurture, and nourishment.

In Dad's last seven years his humanity, life and vitality drifted away. He was afflicted with the debilitating disease, dementia. It was an extremely sad situation. It was excruciating to watch

> someone I had come to know as a great man, my Dad, fade away. At the same time it was exquisite – having some of my warmest conversations with him. John Falzon died in June, 2010
>
> The father factor has been pivotal in my life. It drove me to proactively seek a better relationship with my Dad. I am one of the fortunate ones to have been able to find resolution in my relationship with my Dad in my life time and subsequently be transformed in the process.

The social science research on the importance of fathers is now firmly positioned and convincing. Children do better by almost every common social indicator when they have an involved, loving, and nurturing relationship with both a father and a mother (Allen and Daly, 2007; Erickson, 2011; McLanahan and Sandefur, 1997). Conversely, they tend to do worse in life when they have no fathering or very poor fathering (Jaffe et al, 2003).

The father factor powerfully affects not only sons, daughters and mothers – it also has an influence on society as a whole. Studies in the US have shown that the percentage of fatherless youth in a neighbourhood is one of the best predictors of crime rates for that neighbourhood (Gottfredson and Hirschi, 1990).

> CASE STUDY: In the late 1980s, the elephant population at Kruger National Park in South Africa became unmanageable. It was felt that the only solution was to cull the elephant population and it was the adult elephants that were killed. Some of the young elephants that remained were then transferred to Pilanesburg National Park in the northern part of the country.

> Not long after the transfer of the juvenile elephants, some abnormalities started occurring at the young elephants' new home. Violent killings of white rhinoceroses started occurring. At first the rangers suspected that poachers were responsible, but video footage showed otherwise. The rhinos were being killed by the young male elephants. This was perplexing. The terrorizing of other animals was contrary to normal elephant behavior.
>
> The rangers started to suspect that the natural social order had been upset by the separation of the young elephants from the older ones, so they decided to transfer some older male elephants into Pilanesburg National Park. After this transfer occurred, the young male elephants settled down into normal, non-violent elephant behavior.
>
> The park managers subsequently realized that the problematical behavior of the young elephants had been brought on by musth, a condition of suddenly increased testosterone during mating season. Normally, the younger males' fighting instincts are kept in check by the presence and dominance of the older elephants, but this socializing influence had been taken away with the removal of the older animals. The re-introduction of the older males to the herd created a civilizing influence and restored the natural order.

Based on evidence, data and the insights provided by pertinent case studies, this book will argue that fathers and father-child relationships matter. The influence of fathers forms an indelible impression on the lives of children. Good fathering grows healthy children, it fosters stable marriages and it forms the scaffolding of a robust and strong society.

The father factor can be either a positive or negative influence in our lives, and it is within our power to make it a positive one. If we forego anger towards our fathers for their failings, and if we express gratitude for the contribution they made to our lives, we unlock a door which leads to a happier life (Worthington, E, 2004).

This is the father factor. It is real, it is relevant, and it is destiny shaping.

1.1 Book outline

The remainder of this book consists of nine chapters. Chapter 2 provides some historical context along with some public stories to explain and exegete the message of *The father factor*. Chapter 3 looks at the evidence on what drives happiness and success in life. Not surprisingly, the childhood relationships between children and parents are seen to be among the pivotal factors. Chapter 4 looks at the positive ways in which fathers influence the lives of their offspring. Chapter 5 discusses the very real problems of poor fathering and poor responses to fathering. Chapter 6 considers what children can do to initiate recovery from poor childhood relationships with parents. Chapter 7 explores how parents can help to repair the damage from broken parent-child relationships. Chapter 8 looks at the importance of the father-mother relationship for children. Chapter 9 considers the evidence for the role that spirituality can play in overcoming the effects of an impoverished childhood. Chapter 10 presents conclusions.

Appendix I incorporates stories from some of the men and women we have met on our journey. Appendix II presents details for some of the evidence presented in the main body of the book. Finally, Appendix III includes a selection of resources and information for developing and advocating healthy fatherhood.

Throughout the main body of this book, we, the authors, have generally tried to restrict our claims to what could be supported by empirical studies. We have, though, included various personal stories and case studies which have allowed people to give voice to their experiences, largely unedited.

2

The father factor

"It is easier for a father to have children than for children to have a real father." *Angelo Roncalli*

In the 31 years that I (Robert) have been married to my wife, Alicia, we have given birth to four children – Isaac, Matthias, Chiara and Shem. The joys of fatherhood have been many. When I set out on the great adventure of fathering, however, I had no comprehension of what it would take to be the father I desired and dreamed to be. Nor did I know how I would go about fulfilling the great responsibility of raising sons and daughters into men and women.

I was ill-equipped, idealistic and naïve – no training, no plan, no method, no instructions, no tools and no real sense of the staggering impact and generational imprint I would make in the most important task and vocation ever to be assigned to me. How would I do fathering? I received more instructions on how to set up our new blue ray DVD player with its two manuals (one written in five languages), warranties and a help-line, than anything that I had been given to be a father. This was like some high school science experiment where at any time something might just explode. Like it or not, my children were a great genealogical experiment.

I am not alone in my lack of training for effective fatherhood. This book has been written, in part, to help fathers to be better informed about their vitally important vocation. The book has also been written with a view to helping sons, daughters, mothers and society restore the ground lost to them from poor father-child relationships.

2.1 Fatherhood – the good and the bad

Fatherhood has become increasingly complex to define and discuss as man's role in family life has changed. There are many sensitive pressure points in any discussions around fathers, fatherhood and fathering. Often the conversations uncover some very raw wounds, yielding a mixed array of emotions, opinions and stories.

This book defines fathers to be males who bring forth life in children. That life can be physical, emotional, cognitive, moral or spiritual. Fathers can be biological parents, but they need not be so. All who are male adults have the ability to father.

The book discusses both the wounding and the wonders of fatherhood via evidence, stories and case studies. This book celebrates the fact that at its best, fathering is heroic, loving, wise, nurturing, protective, providing and formative, with wonderful outcomes.

> CASE STUDY: In his book, *Fathers keep their promises*, Scott Hahn recounts the story of an Armenian man who lived through an earthquake in his town. After the earthquake struck, his son's school was reduced to a pile of rubble.
>
> After hearing about the traumatic event, the father rushed to his son's school and started pulling the bricks and rubble away, even though the scene looked hopeless. Few tried to

> help him and many of those who did assist gave up after a while. Some just told him "They're all dead".
>
> The father kept digging away, until incredibly, after 38 hours of digging, he heard a dim cry from his son ... "Papa". The excited father kept digging and eventually pulled his son to safety. His son was saved, and so were 32 others because of the father's love and determination.

This book also acknowledges that at their worst, fathers can be horrifically harmful: neglectful, abusive, violent, absent and substance-dependant. This can beget very negative outcomes for children, marriages and society. A very poor father actually tends to be worse than no father at all (Jaffe et al, 2003). This book discusses this sad reality, presenting the bad news as well as the good.

While good fathering can occur in various places and ways, it tends to flourish most easily within a stable, happy marriage between a cohabitating father and mother (Andrews, 2012). Commenting on the advantage of the two parent family over a single parent one, Urie Bronfenbrenner, an influential Professor of Developmental Psychology at Cornell University, has stated that (Bronfenbrenner, 1990):

> Controlling for associated factors such as low income, children growing up in [single-parent] households are at greater risk for experiencing a variety of behavioural and educational problems, including extremes of hyperactivity or withdrawal; lack of attentiveness in the classroom; difficulty in deferring gratification; impaired academic achievement; school misbehaviour; absenteeism; dropping out; involvement in socially alienated peer groups; and, especially, the so-called 'teenage syndrome' of behaviours that tend to hang together – smoking, drinking, early and frequent

sexual experience, a cynical attitude to work, adolescent pregnancy, and in the more extreme cases, drugs, suicide, vandalism, violence, and criminal acts.

2.2 Demographic trends

Sadly, various demographic wedges have occurred in recent decades to undermine the very environment where fatherhood tends to flourish most easily – the stable marriage environment. According to the work in (Bachrach and Sonenstein, 1998), these demographic wedges have been:

i) reduced marriage rates,
ii) increased marital instability, and
iii) increased child-bearing out of wedlock.

The data on family makeup reveals that these key demographic changes first started to gain a foothold during the 1960s. See, for example, Figure 1, which shows the percentage of American houses headed by sole females between 1960 and 2012 (Solomon-Fears et al, 2013). The number of father absent homes tripled between 1960 and 2012.

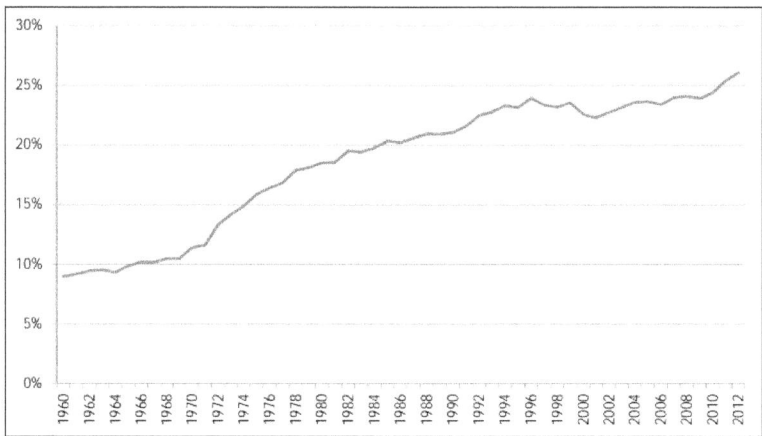

Figure 1. Percentage of sole female led houses in the US (1960-2012).
Source: Congressional Research Service (CRS), based on data from the US Census Bureau

The rise in fatherless homes was most rapid in the 1970s. Interestingly, many of the parents who separated during the 1970s were born during the 1940s. Perhaps the traumas of a world war and the absence of their fathers during that war scarred many children and left them ill equipped to function as confident parents themselves. Perhaps there was undue influence from a very powerful emerging mass media. Perhaps the apparent freedoms offered by the sexual revolution lessened commitment to the family. Perhaps there were other factors which undermined the stability of the family unit.

Regardless of why so many fathers have been separated from their children, there is now a significant problem facing society. The physical absence of fathers and the poor quality of many father-child relationships has caused problems for children in myriad ways.

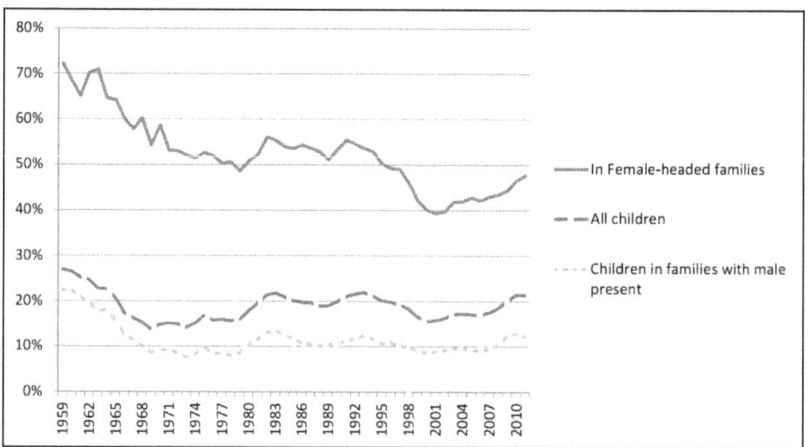

Figure 2. Poverty rates for different types of US families.
Source: Congressional Research Service (CRS), based on data from the US Census Bureau

One very telling way that father absence has affected children is through the mechanism of reduced financial provision (Solomon-Fears et al, 2013). Single parenthood and divorce tend to strongly engender poverty – although it is also true that poverty tends to cause divorce and single parenthood. The child poverty problem in father absent homes is highlighted in Figure 2, which shows the poverty rates for various types of American households between 1959 and 2011. Households led by sole females are seen to have poverty rates that are more than four times as great as those with a male adult present.

The past 50 years have also seen a rapid rise in crime rates. See Figure 3, for example, which shows the incarceration rates between 1925 and 2010 in the US.

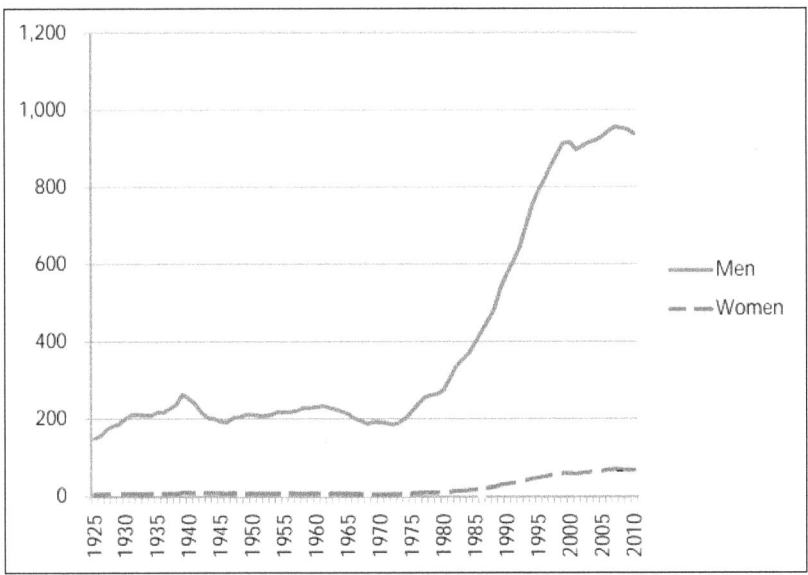

Figure 3. Incarceration rates of American children (1925 to 2010).
Source: Congressional Research Service (CRS), based on data from the University of Albany Sourcebook of Criminal Justice Statistics

There are many factors contributing to the rise in crime rates, and the dearth of fatherly care appears to be one of them. Even after controlling for plausible confounding factors, it has been found that youth in fatherless families are more than twice as likely to be incarcerated as their counterparts in intact two parent families (Harper and McLanahan, 2004).

Other factors which appear to be contributing to the rise in crime rates are family instability and family reconstitution. These may pose an even bigger risk than father absence. It has been found, for example, that youth from families comprised of a father and a stepmother are almost four times as likely to be incarcerated as those from intact two parent families (Harper and McLanahan, 2004; see also Section 2 of Appendix II). Of course, these studies show only trends. The vast majority of children from fatherless and re-constituted families have not been incarcerated. Nonetheless, children from these types of families do often face greater challenges in life.

The message of *The father factor* is that father-child relationships matter. They help to mould our destiny. The demise of these relationships has robbed many people of important life advantages. The poor state of many father-child relationships constitutes a social crisis which began decades ago and of which we are now suffering the deepening consequences.

2.3 The good news

The good news presented in Chapters 6 to 9 of this book is that there are solutions and restorative strategies which work. With the appropriate attitudes and proactive action, it is possible for an individual to reclaim the ground lost from deficient father-child relationships. It is also possible for responsible communities to reverse the societal trend of deteriorating fatherhood and the consequences thereof. These solutions are by no means quick fixes – they require perseverance and courage, but they bring great rewards.

CASE STUDY: Concerned about the damaging effect of fatherlessness on its citizens, the town of Chattanooga in the US decided in 1997 to take remedial action. A group of private businesses within the town launched the 'First Things First' project. They had three goals:

i)   to reduce fatherlessness,
ii) to reduce divorce rates and
iii) to reduce unwed pregnancies,

all by 30% within 10 years. The businesses used their financial and human resources to:

i)   provide education,
ii) foster collaboration, and
iii) mobilise the citizens of the town in the cause of family life.

They set up a web-site (//firstthings.org/), organised seminars and provided resources and support. After 15 years the divorce rate in the town had dropped by 27%, the teen unwed pregnancy rate had dropped by 63% and fatherly involvement in families had significantly increased.

2.4 Summary

- All adult males have the potential to father (bring forth physical, emotional, cognitive, moral or spiritual life in children).
- Good fathers tend to cast a very positive influence on children, while very poor fathering can be quite destructive.
- Good fathering can occur in many ways but tends to flourish most easily in families with loving co-resident mothers and fathers.
- There were major demographic trends which began during the 1960s, and which separated many fathers from their families. These changes were i) reduced marriage rates, ii) increased marital instability and iii) increased out of wedlock births.
- The increase in absent fathers and poor fathering has been accompanied by problems with reduced financial provision, increased crime rates and various other social problems.
- Individuals and societal groups have the power to turn the father factor from a negative influence into a positive one.

3

The key drivers of success and happiness

The research evidence has much to teach us about success, happiness and health. Some of this evidence was provided in the Grant Study of Adult Development, one of the longest ever prospective studies. It followed 268 sophomore men studying at Harvard over a period of seven decades (Vaillant, 1977; Vaillant, 2002; Vaillant, 2012). Among these men was US President, John F. Kennedy.

The Grant Study was originally undertaken in 1939 to gain information on healthy ageing. It has garnered much attention largely because it has been one of the few studies to analyse not just short-term effects, but also long-term effects. The latter are prolific in nature, and studies which overlook them can miss critically important links. Over the course of the Grant Study the participants were evaluated every two years by surveys and by examination of medical and financial records. Interviews were also conducted throughout the duration of the study.

3.1 Happiness and success

The Grant Study produced a number of important findings about long-term happiness and success.

The relationship (or love) factor

The first key finding was that the relationship (or love) factor was a very strong predictor of happiness and success (Vaillant, 2012; Vaillant, 2013). The depth of love and the breadth of love were both important.

Inter-generational love was found to be particularly significant. People who were caring for subsequent generations of children at age 50, for example, were three to six times as likely to be happy in old age as those who were not (Vaillant, 2012).

While it may be intuitively obvious that love is important for happiness, the connection between love and success may not be so clear. Yet the findings of the Grant Study were strong in this area. On average those who were ranked in the top category for 'warmth of relationships' earned a maximum lifetime wage which was 2.4 times as great as that of the men ranked in the bottom category (Vaillant, 2012; Vaillant, 2013). The men in the top category for 'warmth of relationships' averaged a maximum lifetime wage of $243,000, while those in the bottom category averaged $102,000.

It is not certain how the relationship factor influences financial success. Perhaps those who love deeply work hard so that they can provide for those they love, and this hard work fosters success. Perhaps those with good relationship skills are valued by employers. Perhaps there are other mechanisms.

The warmth of relationships was found in the Grant Study to correlate with financial success much more than IQ or socio-economic status. Men who had an IQ between 110 and 125 had roughly the same maximum life income as those with IQs above 150. (Stossel, 2013).

The mother factor

A second key finding of the Grant Study was that the warmth of relationships in childhood was a good (though not infallible) predictor of the warmth of relationships later in life.

The warmth of the childhood relationship with the mother (i.e. the mother factor) was found to be a strong long-term predictor of financial success and work success. On average, men who had warm childhood relationships with their mothers earned a maximum lifetime wage of $87,000 per year more than those with cold childhood relationships with their mothers (Vaillant, 2013). The relationship with the father (i.e. the father factor) did not predict financial success nearly as well as the mother factor.

A British study also found that the mother had a significant influence on a child's future financial success. Flouri and Buchannan followed a group of English males who went on to become manual workers in their adult lives. The investigators found that increased involvement of the mother (but not the father) in early childhood correlated with increased employment prospects in adulthood (Flouri and Buchannan, 2002).

> CASE STUDY: In 1997 *Life Magazine* provided a subjective list of the 100 most influential people in the previous 1000 years of world history. The magazine ranked Thomas Edison at the top of the list.
>
> The magazine elevated Edison to such an esteemed position because he dramatically changed the way people lived. He took civilisation from the Steam Age into the Electrical Age. Edison invented the electric light bulb; he developed the world's first practically viable electrical power distribution system; he invented the first sound recording device and he co-invented the first motion picture film camera. Through the

many inventions he patented and the companies he set up, Edison acquired enormous wealth.

What drove Edison to achieve so much and to acquire so much wealth? According to Edison himself, it was his relationship with his mother. He claimed that:

"My mother was the making of me. She was so true and so sure of me, and I felt I had something to live for, someone I could not disappoint".

While he was still a young adult, Edison's mother developed a mental illness and it grieved him to see the mother he loved suffering. He said as a young adult that he was determined to become a successful inventor so that he could provide for his mother financially and improve her diminishing quality of life.

CASE STUDY: In 1847 Alexander Graham Bell was born in Scotland to parents Alexander and Eliza. As an adult, Bell devised one of the most financially lucrative inventions of all time – the telephone. In 1888 the patent rights for this invention were estimated to be worth $25 million.

The key to the invention of the telephone was the development of a sensor which could convert acoustical vibrations into electrical ones. This was vital because electrical vibrations could be transmitted over much longer distances than acoustical ones.

Why was it that Bell was able to devise the critically important sensor before his many eminent competitors? It was partly because he had been working on acoustically related sensor

> techniques since he was a boy. His interest was piqued by his relationship with his mother. She started to go deaf when he was only twelve and Alexander went to great lengths to deduce sensing techniques that could help her to grasp what people were saying.
>
> Bell used to sit by his mother's side while the family was talking and convey the conversations to her via a manual finger tapping language. He also discovered that if he spoke in certain modulated tones into his mother's forehead, she could pick up the vibrations and understand what he was saying.
>
> Bell's efforts to help his mother stimulated a life-long interest in acoustic sensing, which eventually bore fruit in the development of the telephone.

Men who had warm relationships with their mothers were additionally found to be significantly less likely to develop dementia late in life (Stossel, 2013).

The father factor

A third key finding of the Grant Study was that the father factor strongly predicted long-term happiness and marital success. It was, in fact, a much better predictor of long-term happiness and marital success than the mother factor. Good father-child relationships appeared to enhance the ability to play. At age 75, men who had warm childhood relationships with their fathers were less anxious, enjoyed vacations more and had higher life satisfaction levels than those who did not (Stossel, 2013).

CASE STUDY: Nikola Tesla was a contemporary of Thomas Edison and his creative genius and work ethic were comparable to Edison's. Tesla invented the induction motor, the Tesla coil, a remote controlled boat, and contributed very significantly to the invention of radio. Arguably his most famous contribution to technology was the development of alternating current (AC) electrical distribution systems.

Tesla lived a very colourful life. During his time studying at the Austrian Poltechnic in Graz, he developed an addiction to gambling and failed his university examinations. He left the university and severed all ties with his family to conceal the fact that he had dropped out of university. Many of his friends even thought he had died. Tesla's father pleaded with his son to return home but he refused. Tesla had difficulty coping with all of these problems and suffered a nervous breakdown.

Some years later Tesla went to America and worked for Edison. In due course the two men had a very serious and very public falling out. Their conflict was an enduring one, although Edison eventually offered something of an olive branch by acknowledging that he had mistreated Tesla and failed to respect him. Tesla, however, struggled to forgive, even after Edison had died. Upon Edison's death Tesla wrote a scathing criticism of his former employer which was printed in the *New York Times*. It was in stark contrast to all the other commentaries on Edison that appeared there.

Although Tesla's gifts and industry were comparable to Edison's, he appeared to have greater struggles with his addictions and with his relationships with his parents. He also

> chose a predominantly asocial existence, focusing instead on his work.
>
> It is sad, but perhaps not surprising, to find that Tesla did not fare as well as Edison in amassing long-term wealth or in achieving happiness. Though he was an immensely successful technological innovator, Tesla died alone, poor and in debt.

The addiction factor

A fourth finding of the Grant Study was that addictions such as alcoholism and smoking begat a multitude of damaging outcomes. Alcoholism frequently preceded the trouble in men's lives – 57% of the marriages in the Harvard cohort ended when one of the spouses gave in to alcoholism. Depression usually followed alcoholism, not the other way round.

About 50% of those addicted to alcohol recovered, and a remarkably high percentage of these did so with the help of Alcoholics Anonymous (AA) (Gillis, 2012; Powell, 2012). Many other studies have also looked at the evidence for the effectiveness of AA and Section I of Appendix II reviews those findings.

Smoking and alcoholism also strongly predicted poor physical health in old age. They were, in fact, the two strongest predictors of poor long-term health found in the Grant Study.

The sibling factor

A fifth key finding of the study was that sibling relationships matter. The men who had good sibling relationships when they were young earned a maximum lifetime wage of $51,000 per year more (on average) than those with poor sibling relationships (Vaillant, 2013).

The resilience factor

A sixth key finding of the study was that what goes right in a person's childhood is more important than what goes wrong. If, for example, the men had close, warm relationships with a small number of people in an otherwise dysfunctional family, they often coped relatively well in the long-term (Gillis, 2012).

The restoration factor

A seventh key finding of the study was that dramatic change is possible and it is never too late to find happiness. Adults can escape from the patterns of unhappy childhoods, although it may take substantial time. The Grant Study found that one of the saddest people at the start of the study ended up one of the happiest.

To achieve significant change it was found that one had to adopt the right attitudes and one needed to be persevering. Those who did change for the better tended to embrace forgiveness towards those who had hurt them. This enabled them to 'move on'. Those who successfully changed also tended to be grateful and worked with what they had. They turned 'lemons into lemonade'. They developed a high empathic capacity. That is, they took the time to imagine what others were thinking and feeling. They had a persistent hope and were trusting enough to 'let people in' (Vaillant, 2002; Vaillant, 2012).

3.2 Related studies

The investigators on the Grant Study realised that the cohort of men they chose was not necessarily representative of the general population. They therefore engaged with two additional cohorts for the purposes of study. One was a group of working class inner city men in the Boston area (the Glueck Study) and the other was a group of gifted women from California (the Terman Study). These extra groups did generally provide validation for the Grant Study results, although they also provided some points of difference. The findings on career success for the men of the Grant Study, for example, did not generalise to the women of the Terman Study (Vaillant, 2002). This difference, though, is not surprising, given that women in the first half of the twentieth century tended to have very different career goals from the men of the time.

> CASE STUDY: Among all the subjects in the Grant, Glueck and Terman Studies, the one who scored the highest in the category of positive ageing was a woman referred to as Iris Joy (Vaillant, 2002). She scored a perfect 15/15.
>
> Iris did not smoke or drink. She had a wonderful relationship with her parents. She had no formal university education, but was an avid reader and had educated herself. She married young to a man she described as being "such a fun guy" and her marriage of 45 years was very happy. When asked if she ever came close to divorce she replied "Divorce, never – murder, yes" with characteristic good humour.
>
> She and her husband found creative ways to forgive one another and to turn 'lemons into lemonade'. If she became too heated during one of their fights, her husband would send her down the road to visit Mandy, her friend. Mandy had eight unruly children and after spending a couple of hours with them Iris would realise how lucky she was and would want to go home.
>
> Her husband would also leave the house if he got mad, and would often come back with pineapple or chocolate. He did not say much when he came back but Iris did not mind. She encouraged him. She said that there was nothing so good as a double bed for settling an argument.
>
> She had an excellent relationship with her siblings. After her husband died, her younger brother came to have dinner with her almost every night of the week.

> When asked what she enjoyed most about retirement she said "Being with children". She delighted in raising her own son and then her grandchildren and then her great grand-children. She also helped to care for many of her nephews, nieces and even the children and old people in her neighbourhood.
>
> The Grant Study found that the quality of one's relationships was the strongest single predictor of success and happiness and Iris Joy exemplified this admirably. Her life abounded in very deep and very broad relationships of love.

3.3 Healthy physical ageing

The Grant Study also investigated the factors which contributed to good physical health in old age. Several key factors were found to be important (Vaillant, 2002).

No smoking or stopping young

The strongest predictor of healthy physical ageing was not being a heavy smoker before the age of 50. If a man had smoked more than a pack a day for at least 30 years since his college years, he was 10 times more likely to die prematurely. Interestingly, though, if a man gave up smoking before the age of 45, there was no discernible effect at age 70. Smoking appeared to affect only physical health, not psychological well-being.

No alcohol abuse

The second strongest predictor of healthy physical ageing was the absence of alcohol abuse. This factor was a powerful predictor of both psychological well-being and physical well-being.

Exercise

Some level of exercise helped to improve both physical and psychological health in old age.

A non-obese body shape

A non-obese body shape was a moderate predictor of physical health in old age, but not psychological health.

Education

Education correlated quite strongly with good health in old age. Education seemed to be important mainly because of the way it fostered self-care and perseverance.

It is possible that education also improved physical health by training people to be life-long learners. This is important because the physical life span of brain cells is extended if people continue to learn new skills throughout their entire life (Gould, 2000).

Warm relationships and a stable marriage

A track record of warm relationships was found to be good for long-term physical and psychological health, as was a stable marriage.

The Grant Study, while very important, is just one study. It is essential to also look at other studies. There are many such studies and they will be explored throughout the remainder of the book.

3.4 Summary

- Relationships of love are pivotally important, and inter-generational relationships are particularly important.
- The breadth of relationships and the quality of relationships are both important.
- Fathers and mothers are both very influential but they appear to have different types of influence. The warmth of mother-child relationships correlates strongly with financial success, while the warmth of father-child relationships correlates strongly with long-term happiness and life satisfaction.
- There is a significant correlation between sibling relationships and success in life.
- What goes right in a person's life is more important than what goes wrong.
- If persistent problems exist, there is a strong possibility that the root cause is a poor relationship with a parent or an addiction or both.
- There is a strong correlation between participation in Twelve Step recovery programs and successful recovery from addictions.
- Regular exercise is important for healthy aging, as is a healthy body shape.
- A stable marriage and warm relationships help to foster happiness and health.
- Life-long learning and education foster improved health.
- Dramatic recovery from additions or emotional problems is possible, although it tends to take time.

4

The role of fathers

"By profession, I am a soldier and take pride in that fact. But I am prouder – infinitely prouder – to be a father. A soldier destroys in order to build; the father only builds, never destroys. The one has the potentiality of death; the other embodies creation and life." *Douglas Macarthur*

Fathers and mothers matter – they strongly affect the way their children's lives unfold. Positive life outcomes are most likely to flow to children if they are lovingly nurtured by both a mother and father (Allen and Daly, 2007; McLanahan and Sandefur, 1997; Vaillant, 2012).

The key calling of a father is to work with the mother to help his children develop a capacity to love and be loved. Fathers are not without natural support in this calling. There are powerful chemical processes in place which help fathers to rise to their responsibilities.

When children are born the neuro-modulating chemicals, vasopressin and oxytocin, are released in fathers and mothers (Freeman, 1995). These chemicals have a number of potent effects. Firstly, they foster a strong sense of love towards the new-born child. For this reason they are often referred to as the 'love drugs'. Secondly, their release triggers a massive clearing of neuronal connections in the brain. This massive re-wiring of the brain paves the way for a comparatively effortless re-orientation of thinking and acting. If fathers and mothers co-operate with these chemical releases they are empowered to think and act in new ways which convey great love to their children.

Although oxytocin and vasopressin are extremely powerful chemicals, they are not deterministic. That is, parents retain their free will and can either accept or reject the chemical influence. So although oxytocin and vasopressin are invaluable props provided by nature to engender love in word and deed, fathers and mothers can freely choose whether or not to take advantage of these props (Zak, 2012).

Fathers and mothers can exploit the power of oxytocin and vasopressin in many different ways. The activities which stimulate the release of these 'love drugs' are:

i) wholesome, affectionate touch (Morhenn, 2012),
ii) eye contact (Gamer et al, 2010; Guastella et al, 2010),
iii) community building activities such as singing and dancing (Freeman, 1996),
iv) joke telling and laughter (Zak, 2012),
v) thrilling communal activities such as theme park visits (Zak, 2012), and
vi) breastfeeding (Stuart-Macadam and Dettwyler, 1995).

If fathers and mothers are affectionate, make frequent eye contact, play, sing, dance, joke and engage in thrilling activities with their children, they can go a long way to teaching their children how to give and receive love. Regular sexual intercourse between the mother and father also stimulates oxytocin release and helps to create a bond which strengthens the family unit (Blaicher et al, 1999; Murphy et al, 1987). Breastfeeding additionally helps the child to develop trust.

CASE STUDY: When Rick Hoyt was born, his umbilical cord accidentally wrapped round his neck and caused major brain damage to occur. His parents were told by doctors that their son would remain a vegetable all his life. Rick's father, Dick, did not believe the doctors, nor did his wife, Judy. They related to their son as a normal human, not as a vegetable. They made eye contact with him, told him jokes and used a lot of physical touch. As they did this they noticed that their son responded.

In time, Dick approached an Engineering School in Boston to see if they could provide some form of assisted communication device to help Rick. The university initially refused because they believed the boy's brain was not functional enough. When they refused Dick asked the Engineering School staff to tell a joke, and when they did Rick laughed. Amazed at the response, the university reconsidered and eventually produced a device which allowed Rick to control a cursor by pressing his head against a switch.

With the apparatus provided by the university, Rick could at last communicate. The first words he pressed into the computer were "Go the Bruins" [a Boston Hockey Team].

Some time later, Dick participated in an endurance race with his son, pushing Rick in a wheelchair. The race was difficult for the father because he was overweight and unfit. After the event Rick said that he enjoyed the race so much that while it was being run he did not feel like he was handicapped. This posed a huge dilemma for Dick – he realised that he could bring forth more life in his son by regularly participating in these types of events, but he knew that it would be difficult, given how unfit he was.

Dick was conflicted, but committed to becoming fit to help

> his son. He later recalled that "Making Rick happy was the greatest feeling in the world." Father and son formed 'Team Hoyt' and became regulars on the endurance circuit. By April, 2014, they had competed in 1,108 endurance events, including six Ironman triathlons and 72 marathons. Dick also cycled and ran across America with his son in 1992, covering 3,735 miles in just 45 days.
>
> Rick's father and mother used the natural prompts of laughter, eye contact and physical touch to initially communicate love to their son. Eventually, his father used some additional artificial technological prompts to help bring forth further life. Finally, Dick co-operated with the oxytocin/vasopressin releases within him to radically change the way he thought and acted. Ultimately he brought forth a measure of life within his son that had been deemed inconceivable by the medical authorities.

Nurture and play

Fathers and mothers often express their love by spending large amounts of time caring for, talking to, and playing with their children. The father's love and the mother's love do not always manifest in the same way, though. Studies indicate that young children prefer to receive caregiving and comfort from the mother, while they prefer to play with the father (Lamb, 1997). The mother tends to differ from the father in the level of sensitivity that she offers in her caregiving. Mothers tend to be more aware of distress in children.

There are five particular ways in which the father's play tends to differ from that of the mother (Rowe et al, 2004). Firstly, fathers tend to use a more roughhouse style of play, which prompts children to develop greater control of their bodies and emotions. Secondly, fathers tend to encourage children to take more risks, both when they play and when they navigate through life. This emboldens them to successfully negotiate life's many challenges. Thirdly, fathers tend to use more questioning in their talk with young children. They tend to use words such as "what" and "where" more frequently and this tends to elicit greater interactivity from children. As a result children tend to talk more, use more extensive vocabulary and use longer sentence structures. Fourthly, fathers tend to inculcate a strong sense of protection and children who spend a lot of time with fathers tend to be less vulnerable to sexual abuse or assault. Fifthly, fathers tend to provide firmer discipline, whereas mothers tend to incorporate more negotiation in their discipline. Both forms are important, with the firmer discipline providing the groundwork to be able to push through pain barriers and achieve major goals.

4.1 The quality of fatherly involvement

While involved fathers have considerable influence on their children, not all forms of fatherly involvement are equally effective. The literature suggests that the most effective form is 'authoritative parenting'. This type of parenting involves:

i) listening, encouraging, and conveying warmth,
ii) providing/offering everyday assistance,
iii) providing reasonable and consistent discipline and
iv) facilitating increased independence in children over time.

Amato and Gilbreth established the importance of authoritative parenting with a meta-analysis published in 1999. In their meta-analysis, they compared four key aspects of fatherhood among non-resident fathers – feelings of closeness, frequency of contact, payment of child support and authoritative parenting (Amato and Gilbreth, 1999). They found that the most consistent predictor of positive child outcomes was authoritative parenting.

Many non-resident fathers appear particularly prone to recoiling from authoritative parenting. Such fathers often participate in leisure activities with their children but fail to fulfil other important duties such as talking about problems and setting boundaries (Amato and Gilbreth, 1999). If non-resident fathers do persist effectively in their authoritative parenting, however, the children can often cope relatively well with life.

4.2 Fostering the development of children's potential

Not only do fathers need to love their children, they also need to help them develop their talents and so realise their potential in life. The research on expertise development provides important insights into how this can be best achieved.

Guiding through example

In the first stages of learning humans progress very effectively by seeing and studying examples (Sweller et al, 1998; Tomasello et al, 1993). This is at no time more important than in the first six years of life or the so-called 'critical period'.

At the start of the critical period the region of the child's brain known as the *nucleus basalis* (NB) is 'turned on' (Kilgar et al, 1998). When this occurs the child's attention becomes highly focused in an automatic way, thereby enabling the child to learn with almost no effort. It is for this reason that children below the age of six can learn languages so easily. At the end of the critical period the NB is turned off, and from that time onwards, learning requires significantly more effort.

Because of the heightened attention facilitated by the activation of the NB, the examples of behaviour the child sees during the critical period tend to make a strong and lasting impression. In light of the above, it is particularly important that fathers set a good behavioural example during the first years of children's lives.

The research evidence not only substantiates the importance of providing good examples, it also provides insight into how to provide these examples. Firstly, *many* examples need to be provided – many more than intuition might suggest (Sweller et al, 1998). The use of many examples helps reinforcement to occur in the brain so that learning becomes ingrained and automatic. Secondly, the examples need to be *well varied* so that the one who observes them can abstract enough key underlying principles to cope with a wide variety of real world scenarios (Sweller et al, 1998).

> CASE STUDY: Joel Osteen is one of the most successful writers and teachers in the world. His first book, "Your best life now", debuted at Number 1 on the *New York Times* best-seller list, and went on to sell four million copies. His next four books also became Number 1 best-sellers. When he teaches publicly he regularly packs out large stadiums, both in his native America and abroad.
>
> Joel maintains that his father played a huge part in his becoming a successful teacher. He grew up with a father, John, who loved him dearly and whom he loved in return. John was a gifted teacher and he wanted Joel to follow in his footsteps. Joel, however, had different ideas. As a young adult Joel went off to college to follow his interests in the area of audio and video production.
>
> After studying for some time at college, Joel decided to ask if he could return home and work on the video productions of his father's teaching. His father was happy to have his son back and willingly agreed. When Joel returned he proceeded to work on his father's video productions for 17 years. During that time the father often tried to get Joel to help him do the teaching but Joel consistently refused.

After 17 years, Joel's father, John, developed a serious illness and was taken to hospital. From his hospital bed, John asked Joel if he could fill in for him in one of his teaching engagements. Joel agreed to do so and this first attempt at teaching went well.

Soon after Joel performed his first teaching duty, John died. Before he died, though, the father had taken great consolation in the fact that his son had been successful in his first attempt at teaching.

After his father's death Joel was grief stricken, since he had lost the father whom he loved dearly. Nonetheless he knew he had to carry on with his life. He also felt compelled to continue filling in for his father as a teacher. What happened in the aftermath of John's death was extraordinary. Joel quickly became extremely successful as a teacher and many people came to listen to him and to be mentored by him.

Joel claims that a key factor in his success as a teacher was the training which effectively took place as he produced and edited his father's teaching videos. As Joel compiled these videos he would routinely watch them about four times in order to critically review them. In so doing Joel studied and reflected on many and varied examples of good teaching over a period of 17 years.

Given the evidence on the importance of studying many and varied examples, it is easy to understand why Joel managed to acquire such good teaching skills. These skills were further refined as Joel progressed from the study of teaching to the practice of teaching. They were enhanced even further as he started to mentor others in the area of teaching.

> An additional lesson to be learned from the story of Joel Osteen is the importance of love in training up children. If Joel had not felt such love and acceptance from his father, he probably would not have decided to return from college and work for him. He would also have been unlikely to endure 17 years of studying his father's examples.

Deliberate practice

There comes a point where studying examples is no longer productive, and where it is detrimental to one's development (Kalyuga et al, 1998). At that point it is necessary to move beyond studying examples and actually put those examples into practice.

The social science research reveals that practice is extraordinarily important for expertise development. It is, in fact, far more important than natural talent in the long term (Ericsson et al, 1993). Studies have also shown that not all practice is equally effective for skills development. The kind of practice which is most effective is *deliberate practice* (Ericsson et al, 1993). This is practice which is:

i) driven by a vision,

ii) informed by copious amounts of feedback,

iii) repeated frequently with continual monitoring of performance,

iv) mentally demanding and engaging,

v) characterized by regular striving beyond what has previously been achieved, and

vi) moderated by much creative reflection.

To properly develop our potential in a given area we need to engage in at least 10,000 hours of deliberate practice (Gladwell, 2008). Mozart, Chess Champion, Bobby Fischer, and Bill Gates all engaged in this type of extended deliberate practice before they became famous.

Fathers can help their children's development by encouraging and supporting them in their engagement with deliberate practice. The particular ways they can do this are discussed below.

Fostering good self-discipline

Deliberate practice is mentally demanding (i.e. hard). Good self-discipline is therefore required. Good fathers tend to provide firm discipline which assists children to develop effective self-discipline (Rowe et al, 2004).

Providing feedback

Deliberate practice requires continual feedback on performance. Not all feedback is helpful, however (Hattie, 2009). For the feedback to be effective it must be welcomed by the recipient. The chances of a positive reception to the feedback are enhanced if the recipient believes the one delivering the feedback cares about them. Fathers who care deeply about their children are ideal candidates to deliver the necessary feedback.

Encouraging children to regularly 'push the envelope'

Practicing routine activities is a feature of conventional practice, but not of deliberate practice. The latter is characterised by the regular breaking of new ground and therefore of regular risk-taking. Research suggests that fathers tend to encourage their children to take risks (Rowe et al, 2004).

CASE STUDY: On a family holiday in an Adriatic sea-side town, a young Monica Seles saw her father and brother packing a bag of tennis rackets. She asked them where they were going and her brother said they were going to play tennis. Monica heard the word "play" and that sounded like fun. She asked if she could go with them. They said yes and her passion for tennis was birthed.

Her father, Karolj, had a great love for his daughter and found creative ways to make tennis fun for her. She loved the *Tom and Jerry* cartoon and so he would draw the cartoon character, Jerry, on the ball. Monica would pretend to be Tom and would belt Jerry as he tried to escape.

Karolj lived in Novi Sad, Yugoslavia, at a time when the town's tennis facilities were poor, but he worked with what he had. He strung a net between two cars in a car park to create a makeshift tennis court. On one occasion he also drove 10 hours to acquire a tennis racquet. Though he loved his daughter, he was gracious to others as well and would often applaud her sporting opponents.

Karolj was not a professionally trained tennis coach but he learned what he needed to know to help his daughter. Despite his own lack of training, he coached his daughter to the point where she became World Junior Champion. It was he who taught Monica to hit the ball with both hands on both sides. His nurture helped her to become the youngest ever winner of the French Open tournament and eventually the world's top ranked woman player.

> CASE STUDY: Jim McCartney was a man who loved music, and who played the trumpet and piano. Jim strongly encouraged his two sons, Paul and Michael, to develop their musical talents. As part of this process, Jim would often engage his sons in reflecting on the technical aspects of music being played on the radio. He also regularly took them to music concerts.
>
> Through his father's nurture and guidance, Paul, in particular, captured a vision for making music. This vision launched him into a regime of almost relentless deliberate practice. As a young man Paul and his band members practised their live performances so intensely, they notched up over 1200 performances (comprising about 10,000 hours of practice) within a four year period. At the end of this period, his band, *The Beatles*, became internationally famous.
>
> According to the Guinness Book of Records, Paul went on to become the most successful artist in the history of popular music.
>
> As alluded to in this case study, fathers who encourage their children, engage them in reflection and provide them with regular feedback can have a strong influence on their children's development.

4.3 Nurturing the cognitive development of children

Studies have shown that involved fathers tend to produce children with higher IQs and this effect is evident by the age of three (Yogman, Kindlan, and Earls, 1995). When fathers are actively involved in their children's lives, those children are more likely to be higher academic achievers throughout their lives. That is, they are more likely to enjoy school, expend effort at school and get high grades (Alfaro, Umana-Taylor, and Bamaca, 2006; Howard et al, 2006).

> CASE STUDY: Melville Feynman was heavily involved in the intellectual life of his young son, Richard, from a very early age. Melville delighted in teaching the boy and was always keen to help him to learn new things. Melville tried to coax his son to use his intellect to the fullest and he encouraged him to ask lots of questions. He also tried to make sure his son saw the value in challenging orthodox thinking.
>
> Richard responded very positively to his father's intellectual guidance. As an adult he went on to become one of the highest achievers of the 20th century. He developed a formidable intellectual reputation very early in his life, so much so, that when he gave his first graduate seminar at Princeton University, Albert Einstein and John von Neumann attended.
>
> As a young scientist during World War II, Richard was recruited to work at Los Alamos Laboratories on the ground breaking Manhattan Project. In his later work he introduced the concepts of nanotechnology and quantum computing to much of the world. He won the Nobel Prize for Physics in 1965 for his work on quantum electrodynamics and gained widespread public attention when he explained what had caused the Challenger Space Shuttle disaster.
>
> Feynman also stimulated the intellectual development of others, similarly to the way his father had done with him. Robert Barro studied Physics under Feynman at Caltech. Barro realised that he could not match the intellectual accomplishments of the likes of Feynman in Physics, but still wanted to reach the top of his field. He therefore decided to pursue a career in a different area. He chose Economics and

> eventually went on to achieve his goal of becoming the most heavily cited man in his field.
>
> A 1999 poll of leading physicists ranked Richard Feynman among the Top 10 Physicists of all time.

Children of heavily involved fathers also tend to demonstrate greater competence at work (Amato, 1994; Astone and McLanahan, 1991; Barber and Thomas, 1986).

> CASE STUDY: When Nanneri Mozart was seven her father, Leopold, began to teach her the piano, while her younger brother, Wolfgang, looked on. After a while the young boy started to imitate what he was seeing.
>
> When Wolfgang reached the age of four his father started to give him direct tuition and the boy responded in remarkable fashion. Leopold was Wolfgang's only teacher. He taught the boy not only music but also other academic subjects.
>
> Seeing his children's talent, Leopold decided to put much of his effort into nurturing their gifts at the expense of his own career. He travelled throughout Europe with his children to give them opportunities, often under very difficult circumstances. Nanneri and Wolfgang both reaped the benefits of their father's nurture and both became famous in their own lifetimes.

4.4 Nurturing the emotional and social development of children

If fathers are involved in the care of infant children, those children cope better with new situations and new people; they manage stress better; they are more curious; they are more willing to explore and they exhibit more trust in their explorations (Biller, 1993; Kotelchuck, 1976; Parke and Swain, 1975; Pruett, 1997).

The involvement of a father correlates positively with children's feelings of social competence, overall life satisfaction and self-reported happiness (Dubowitz et al, 2001; Flouri, 2005). On the other hand, the involvement of a father correlates negatively with depression, emotional distress, behaviour problems, neuroticism and emotions of fear, guilt and anxiety (Dubowitz et al, 2001; Easterbrooks and Goldberg, 1990; Field et al, 1995; Formoso et al, 2007; Furstenberg and Harris, 1993; Harris et al, 1998; Zimmerman et al, 1995).

Under the right circumstances, the positive findings on the involvement of a father partially generalise to substitute fathers. For this generalisation to hold, however, the substitute must be trusted and loved. Grandfathers who live with and support a single parent, appear to be particularly good candidates for this type of substitute fathering (Harper and McLanahan, 2004).

The warmth in the relationship between adolescent children and stepfathers also correlates positively with a better sense of well-being, better grades, and better behaviour at school (King, 2006; Yuan and Hamilton, 2006).

It is not only the involvement of the father that matters, it is also the quality of involvement. His levels of love and self-sacrifice are particularly important. These attributes can cast a positive influence on the children even after the father dies.

> CASE STUDY: Early in the twentieth century a young girl was born in Arizona. She grew up in a contented home with her mother and father, but she was traumatised one day when her father failed to come home. Her anxiety grew as the days passed with no sight of him and in fact, he never came home.
>
> As the reality of her father's departure took hold, the girl was gripped by a sense of deep rejection. She had to face the fact that her father had left her and had not even bothered to tell her why. Her world was shattered.
>
> After a considerable period of time, the young girl received a letter. It was from her father. In the letter he explained that some time back he had developed terminal cancer. When he received the diagnosis he had considered his situation and had decided not to put his wife and child through the agony of seeing him suffer and die, so he left.
>
> The father explained in the letter that he was now dead, but that since his diagnosis he had spent his time building a new house, a house which he now wanted his wife and daughter to have. He had built this house for them because he hoped that it would help them to know how much he loved them.
>
> When the young girl went to see the house she was startled. It was a mansion of breathtaking beauty, built like a palace. Her father's determination to sacrifice his own needs for those of his daughter profoundly moved her and a sense of gratitude lingered with her for the rest of her life.

Importantly, there are demonstrated *long-term* social benefits to having a close, warm relationship with a father. If children feel close to their fathers they are more likely to have successful and enduring marriages (Franz et al, 1991; Lozoff, 1974; Risch et al, 2004).

4.5 Nurturing the physical health of children

> CASE STUDY: Theodore Roosevelt Snr was a glass importer and one of New York City's leading philanthropists. According to his son, Theodore Snr "combined strength and courage with gentleness, tenderness and great unselfishness".
>
> Roosevelt Snr knew the importance of helping his children to realise their potential. His son was riddled with sickness and it became clear to Roosevelt Snr that a great deal of effort would be needed to overcome this obstacle. Roosevelt Snr told his son:
>
> "Theodore, you have the mind but you have not the body and without the help of the body the mind cannot go as far as it should. I am giving you the tools but it is up to you to make your body".
>
> His son responded:
>
> "I will make my body".
>
> Roosevelt Snr installed gymnasium equipment in the family home and Theodore Roosevelt Jr immediately began to pursue what he called the "strenuous life". This helped him to realise his potential and he did it very successfully.
>
> When his father and mentor died, Roosevelt Jr wrote that his father had influenced him more than any other person. He also described him as "the greatest man he ever knew". At that point Roosevelt Jr decided to change careers – to one involving public service. He felt that the pursuit of such a career would honour his father. Eventually Roosevelt turned to politics, believing that by changing laws he could work for the betterment of society.

> Roosevelt Snr's efforts as a father bore extraordinary fruit in the life of his son. Roosevelt Jnr became the US President and eventually came to be regarded as one of the greatest presidents in the nation's history. As President, he contributed greatly to the completion of the Panama Canal and he negotiated the end of the Sino-Russian war. For the latter, he won the Nobel Peace Prize.

If children live in households without their fathers, they are more likely to have problems with a variety of physical health issues (Horn and Sylvester, 2002). One key problem in contemporary society is obesity and children who live without a father are more likely to carry excessive weight (Strauss and Knight, 1999).

Studies have also shown that the incidence of asthma is strongly linked to the absence of a father. The effect is particularly strong for children of unmarried parents living apart. Such children are 2.61 times more likely to be diagnosed with asthma (Harknett, 2005).

Additionally, fathers indirectly affect the health of children through their support for the mother and her health. Women who feel emotionally supported by their husbands are more likely to have trouble free pregnancies and deliveries. They are also more likely to have good post-partum experiences (Gjerdingen et al, 1991). Single mothers, on the other hand, are twice as likely as their married counter-parts to have incidences of depression (Cairney et al, 2003). Infant mortality rates in unmarried mothers are also about 1.8 times as high as those for married women (Matthews et al, 2000).

4.6 Nurturing the moral and spiritual development of children

Fathers have a significant influence on the moral behaviour of their children. Statistical association studies have shown that children from non-two parent families have a 10-15% higher delinquency rate than children from two parent families (Wells and Rankin, 1991). The percentage of fatherlessness in a neighbourhood has also been found to be one of the best predictors of crime rates for that neighbourhood (Gottfredson and Hirschi, 1990).

Fathers additionally appear to have a strong influence in the area of their children's sexual engagement. Fathers who disapprove of early sexual activity and communicate with their children on sexual matters tend to have less sexually active teens than fathers who do approve (Guilamo-Ramos et al, 2012).

The sexual engagement of children is not only influenced by the attitudes of fathers towards early sexual engagement, but also by the presence or absence of a father. Girls who grow up without a father are much more likely to have a teen pregnancy (Ellis et al, 2003; Jeynes, 2001). Children of involved fathers also tend to be less vulnerable to sexual abuse and sexual assault (Wilcox and Kline, 2013).

As alluded to already, fathers tend to strongly foster moral development in their children's lives through their engagement (or lack of engagement) in authoritative parenting. However, there may be another indirect means of influence. This influence was suggested in a 2005 newspaper article by Niall Ferguson, a Professor of History at Harvard. Although he is a professing atheist, Ferguson argued in his 2005 article that his native Britain needed to rekindle its religious practice (Ferguson, 2005). He questioned where people would get their moral and ethical framework if they did not get it from the church pews.

There is data to suggest that Ferguson might be correct. A major study done by the National Center for Addiction and Substance Abuse at Columbia University found that teens who did not attend religious services at least once a week were more than four times as likely to use illicit drugs (CASA, 2001).

As suggested above, the religious practice of children correlates with increased regard for the law. Curiously, it has also been found that there is a very strong correlation between a father's religious practice and that of his adult children. A Swiss study found that if a father went to church regularly and the mother did not attend at all, then about 44% of the children went on to attend church regularly as adults, while 22% went on to attend church sporadically (Fertfam, 2000). On the other hand, if a mother went to church regularly but the father did not attend at all, 2% of the children became regular attendees as adults, while 37% became sporadic attendees. More detailed statistics are provided in Section 3 of Appendix II.

Mothers and fathers both play an important role in the lives of their children, but they do not always do it in identical ways. The passing on of religious practice by lived example seems to be one area where fathers have unusually strong influence. This does not mean that children without fathers cannot acquire a strong propensity to actively practise religious faith. A finding from the research is that under the right circumstances, caring and trusted substitute fathers can fill the gap left by an absent biological father (Harper and McLanahan, 2004).

> CASE STUDY: One year, I (Peter) went on a tour with a group of people in a van. One of those who travelled with us was a man whom I had not previously met. I was told that this man had been left as an infant on the door-steps of a house belonging to the religious order of the Christian Brothers.
>
> It became clear to the Christian Brothers who found the baby that the mother had deliberately left the baby in their care. Seeking to honour the mother's will, the brothers decided to raise the baby in their community. The baby grew up with them and when the boy came of age he decided that he would join the Christian Brothers.
>
> One thing I remember very clearly about this man is that

> whenever we would arrive in a new town he would go to one of the town's churches to pray.
>
> It seemed to me that this man had found what he lacked from his natural father in two different places; the first was in the community of mentors where he grew up; the second was in the solace he found through his faith in his 'heavenly father'.

4.7 Providing nurture during adolescence

Certain periods of a person's development are particularly important. The first six years of a person's life, for example, are very critical because of the impressionable nature of the brain during that time. Adolescence is another period in which major changes occur in the brain (Spear, 2000). The presence of a father tends to be quite important at that time.

The physical presence of the father appears to be important for both boys and girls during adolescence. A study at the University of Melbourne found that the simple presence of a father (even without any verbal communication) tends to be associated with reduced likelihood of delinquent behaviour in adolescent boys (Cobb-Clark and Tekin, 1996). Even the presence of an adult male role model (whether it be a biological father or not) tends to be associated with reduced incidences of delinquency in adolescent boys (Cobb-Clark and Tekin, 1996).

The absence of a biological father during adolescence has a different effect on girls. It does not raise the risk of delinquency but it is associated with a heightened risk of early puberty. This is highly problematical because early puberty is linked to a host of negative outcomes such as cancer and depression (Larsen et al, 2003). There is also a heightened risk of teen pregnancy in females who experience early puberty (Belski et al, 1991). Sadly, early puberty has become increasingly common in the last few decades (Biro et al, 2013).

One of the key ways a biological father's presence appears to protect against early puberty in girls is by reducing the probability that non-related adult males (such as step-fathers and male partners) take up residence in the family home. The risk of early puberty is no higher when related adult males (such as fathers and older brothers) reside in the home (Milne and Judge, 2010), but it is significantly higher when non-related males (such as step-fathers) are present (Ellis and Garber, 2000).

It is uncertain at this stage why the presence of step-fathers is linked to early puberty in girls. Further research may provide the answer.

4.8 The other key roles of a father

Fathering is a very diverse phenomenon and it is not possible to encapsulate the totality of fatherly roles in one comparatively brief chapter. We therefore invite the readers at this point to consider and answer the following questions for themselves:

What are the other key roles that a father performs?

What role did your father perform most effectively?

4.9 Summary

- The key role of the father is to collaborate with the mother to engage their children in the receiving and giving of love.
- Physical affection, eye contact, joke telling, playful singing and dancing with children and engaging in thrilling activities all tend to communicate love powerfully.
- The father's involvement tends to strongly influence the long-term emotional, physical, intellectual and moral well-being of his children.
- The father plays an especially strong role in the early years which span conception to six years of age.

- Fathers can help children develop their potential through their example and by encouraging them to engage in much deliberate practice of their gifts and talents.
- The most effective type of fatherly involvement is authoritative parenting, which incorporates listening, encouraging, conveying warmth, daily assistance, consistent discipline and the gradual facilitating of independence.
- There is a strong correlation between a father's religious practice and that of his children in adulthood. The correlation between the religious practice of a mother and that of her adult children is not nearly as strong as that of the father.
- Under the right circumstances, caring and trusted substitute fathers can help to fill the gap left by absent or ineffective fathers.
- There is a significant correlation between father absence during adolescence and delinquency in boys. Even the presence of an adult male during adolescence is associated with a reduced risk of delinquency in boys.
- There is a significant correlation between father absence during adolescence and the onset of early puberty in girls. The early onset of puberty is highly undesirable as it is linked to depression and cancer.

5

Poor fathering and poor responses to fathering

"Not every successful man is a good father – but every good father is a successful man." *Robert Duvall*

5.1 Poor fathering

The presence of a father does not always improve the life of a child. Fathers with high levels of anti-social behaviour actually cause more behaviour problems in the children the longer they stay (Jaffe et al, 2003). Very poor fathering actually appears to be worse than no fathering at all.

Because poor behaviour by fathers can be such a problem, it is important to explore the different ways in which it can manifest. The following sub-sections look at some such ways.

Habitual viewing of pornography

The statistics on the viewing of pornography in the western world are telling. According to one study, about 68% of young adult Danish men view porn at least once a week and about 14% of young adult Danish women do likewise (Hald, 2006). A further 17% of young adult Danish men view porn one to two times per month, while a further 30% of young adult Danish women do so. The 2011 pornographic novel, *Fifty*

Shades of Grey, set a record as the fastest selling paperback ever. *Fifty Shades of Grey* and its two sequels had sold about 90 million copies worldwide by February, 2014.

When men watch porn the reward chemical, dopamine, is often released. The reward mechanism within dopamine causes the viewing of the porn to be strongly reinforced so that viewers are likely to return to watch further porn. If a man does keep returning to watch the porn the body eventually responds by desensitising itself. When this happens the porn no longer provides the same stimulation and the viewer often starts to engage with porn which is more extreme or more unusual. This whole process can easily become addictive (Doidge, 2007).

Another powerful chemical can also be released during sexual stimulation. That chemical is oxytocin, or its close relative, vasopressin (Blaicher et al, 1999; Murphy et al, 1987). This chemical tends to promote bonding with the object of the stimulation, and in the process, facilitates a very substantial and lasting rewiring of the brain. The release of this chemical inside marriage tends to promote a strong and deep bonding between spouses. It is therefore quite a positive phenomenon. Outside of marriage the chemical release can cause a strong bonding to someone else, even a fantasy figure. If this bonding occurs with multiple partners (even so-called porn stars), it can create a destructive pulling effect in multiple different directions.

In light of the above facts, it is not surprising to find that studies show prolonged exposure to pornography has a number of negative effects on family life. These effects include (Zillman, 1984):

i) a decreased respect for long-term monogamous relationships and
ii) a reduced appetite for procreation.

CASE STUDY: One young man grew up in a caring family in the US, and he knew the difference between right and wrong. Nonetheless he started to indulge excessively with sexual fantasies. He had little access to graphic images during high school, but things changed when he arrived at college.

While he was studying at college he was gradually drawn very actively into the world of pornography. He initially struggled to overcome the lure of the porn, but in time he became tired of struggling. Then he convinced himself that there was nothing wrong with what he was doing. He became addicted and in an effort to keep himself stimulated, found himself doing things he would once have thought unimaginable.

Two years after graduating from college he married. He thought that married life would solve his pornographic addiction problems. Sadly, it did nothing of the sort. His problems only increased; now he had to maintain a secret life, one which his wife and parents knew nothing about.

Eventually, his guilt drove him to confess his problems to an unsuspecting wife and family. A counsellor tried to explain the effect that his addiction had on his wife. He said it was as if he had driven a mac truck through a beautiful stained glass window.

The young man went through enormous pain and anguish trying to overcome his addiction. Often he would wake up, knowing that he would succumb to the porn, but just wondering how bad it would be.

Out of a concern for his children and his wife he submitted himself to counselling, he engaged in self-reflection, he joined a Twelve Step program and he eventually managed to bring the addiction under control.

The man in the above case study went through great pain, but happily he managed to turn his life around and his marriage survived. Many others have not been so lucky. One study has suggested that about 56% of American divorce cases involve a claim that one of the partners has an obsessive interest in pornography (Manning, 2004).

Sexual abuse

While the viewing of pornography is destructive to family life, other sexual indulgences can be even more damaging. Sexual abuse, in particular, can be devastating.

When a father is involved in sexual abuse, he is much more likely to be a step-father than a natural father. A study of 930 women in the US found that the chances of being abused by a step-father were about seven times as high as abuse by a biological father (Russell, 1984).

The evidence also suggests that the likelihood of sexual abuse by a father is reduced if:

i) the father is present in the family and heavily involved in caring for the children during the early years of their life (Parker and Parker, 1986),

ii) the mother and the father live together (Finkelhor et al, 1990), and

iii) the father's life is not in a state of chaos (Gordon, 1989).

The above findings are not entirely surprising. One would expect that the early bonding between a father and a child would mitigate any inclination towards abuse. Likewise one would have anticipated that well organised mothers and fathers would both serve a protective role in the family.

Alcohol and drug related dependencies

Chemical addictions, like sexual addictions, can be very damaging. In Australia, alcohol and drug addictions have been linked not only to child neglect, but also to child abuse, violence, workplace absenteeism and drink-driving (Austheal, 2012). Alcohol abuse is also the second most common cause of hospitalisation and preventable death in Australia. Only tobacco abuse causes more preventable deaths and instances of hospitalisation (Austheal, 2012).

Excessive alcohol consumption is no small issue for marriages and family. Studies done in the US suggest that if a partner has alcohol related issues, the likelihood of breakup increases by a factor of four (Alcdiv, 2012). The issue of violence is especially problematical.

> CASE STUDY: In contemporary Australia, there has been a great deal of attention given to the problem of violent attacks by angry young men on innocent victims. These attacks have seriously wounded or killed a number of Australians in recent times. These incidents have stirred much public debate about the issues of alcohol dependency and inadequate fathering.
>
> A story in *The Sunday Telegraph* on 4th January, 2014 profiled the case of a young male who had carried out one of these deadly acts.
>
> The young man was described as fit, strong, angry and partial to drinking. He had apparently taken 24 pre-mixed vodkas to a friend's house before proceeding to kill his victim with a knockout punch.
>
> The judge noted in passing his verdict that:
>
> "The offender grew up in his mother's care and without the benefit of love, support and guidance from his father. ... On one occasion during the offender's childhood, his

> father struck him across the face with a bamboo cane as punishment for a trivial misdemeanour ... He formed a close relationship with his football coach, and I infer from his mother's statement that man may have been something of a father figure to the offender. Unfortunately he died of cancer, which the offender's mother states was very confronting for the offender".
>
> The judge understood the tragic background which may have cultivated the young man's violent streak, but he also understood the need for people to take responsibility for their actions. He sentenced the offender and sent him to prison.

The above case study highlights that there is a social consequence of excessive alcohol consumption. It is not just the alcoholic and their families who suffer – the broader society can suffer as well.

Emotional abuse

Abuse of children can take many forms. It can be physical, sexual, or verbal/emotional. In a large survey in the US 26% of respondents reported having suffered verbal abuse, 15% reported having endured physical abuse and 12% reported sexual abuse (Cdc, 2010).

Verbal and emotional abuse can be characterised by such practices as regular

i) name calling,
ii) insults,
iii) ridicule,
iv) excessive criticism,
v) humiliation,
vi) loud yelling and
vii) destruction of personal property.

Parents can fall into emotional abuse for a variety of reasons. Sometimes they are simply copying the example of their parents, who abused them when they were children. Sometimes emotional abuse flows on from alcohol and drug related problems.

Regardless of the reasons, there are strategies which parents can use to move forward. Some of these strategies are discussed in the following chapter.

Emotional disengagement

Some fathers disengage emotionally from their children by either spending large amounts of time away from home, or by being non-interactive when they are at home.

Those fathers who do spend long hours away from home often do so at work. A strong commitment to work is not itself a problem. If fathers involve their children in their work, very positive outcomes can flow from that (Robinson, 2001). The difficulty comes when there is no involvement of children in the father's professional life and work is used as a wedge between the father and the children. Sadly, many contemporary western fathers see the workplace as being a 'child-free zone'. This unfortunate attitude started to gain real traction during the industrial revolution, when the economy changed from being largely farm and shop based, to one based on industrialisation. With this transition, many fathers moved en-masse from the family farms and shops into the urban factories.

Interestingly, the workplace environment has changed in recent times with the development of the internet and it is possible for many fathers to work (at least in part) at home. This creates a significant opportunity for reversing the trend which set in with the industrial revolution. There is real potential to restore a culture of better fathering.

When fathers recoil from interaction in the home it is often done by spending large amounts of time watching TV. There are a number of problems with this kind of behaviour. Firstly, time spent watching TV takes away from time relating in a more interactive way with other family members. Secondly, excessive TV watching provides a poor example for children to follow.

Young children can ill afford to start watching large amounts of TV. If they do so they are at increased risk of obesity (Gortmaker et al, 1996). Television is also rife with violence and sexual content. Unless there is strict monitoring, these components can adversely affect the development of young children.

5.2 Poor responses to fathering

Un-forgiveness and judgment

Very poor behaviour by fathers has a negative long-term impact on sons and daughters in many, but not all, instances. The father's offspring can avoid negative long-term consequences if they make decisions to refrain from responding negatively to their father's poor behaviour – that is, if they decide not to give in to un-forgiveness and other destructive attitudes.

The emotional, physical and mental health of a son or daughter are all undermined by negative attitudes such as un-forgiveness towards parents (Linden and Maercker, 2011; Worthington, E, 2004). The power of forgiveness becomes apparent when one compares the long-term well-being of children who lose their father through death with the well-being of children who lose their father through divorce or abandonment. Children who lose their father through death tend to be less disadvantaged in the long-term. One study showed, for example, that about 15% of children who lost their father through death dropped out of school prematurely, compared with about 13% for intact families. By contrast, 31% of children from divorced families dropped out prematurely, as did 37% of children born out of wedlock (McLanahan and Sandefur, 1997).

It must be acknowledged that there are often very real and painful consequences of losing a father through death (Berlinsky and Biller, 1982), but the negative long-term effects are not usually as great as those which accrue from divorce or abandonment.

The comparatively lesser damage done to the children by the death of a father can be explained by the fact that the children typically have little reason to blame or judge their father when he dies. Often, in fact, these children focus on an idealised memory of their father, which casts a positive influence on them well after the father's death.

Children who have lost a father because of abandonment or divorce can achieve relatively good outcomes in life if they refrain from (or retract) judgment toward their father and focus on his positive contributions. This, of course, may be quite challenging, but is likely to reap large rewards. It is also important to note that it is never too late to change attitudes towards a father. These kinds of attitude changes can strongly affect a person's destiny.

Rebellion

Sometimes sons and daughters undermine the relationship with their father even when there is no bad behaviour on the part of the father. He may simply have disciplined them or made legitimate demands of them and they have responded with rebellion. This rebellion can make life difficult for the father and impair his ability to impart love.

> CASE STUDY: Alicia Beth Moore, commonly known as the rock star, PINK, said in an interview with Andrew Denton on Enough Rope:
>
> "Well my dad left and then I figured out that I had a lot more freedom without him there and the house was a more peaceful place without them fighting all the time. So I did a lot of drugs, ran away from home and pretty much lost my mind.

> Up until I was about 15 years old when my mum kicked me out, dropped out of high school, had a record deal six months later and haven't touched a drug since Thanksgiving of '95".
>
> Then later in the interview she said:
>
> "I don't believe in regrets. I have one regret; that when my mum kicked me out of the house I had an opportunity to spend some time with my dad but I was so gone at that point that I wasted six months of my life that I could have spent with my dad; but everything happens for a reason. I think that's my one regret in my whole life".

A failure to use gifts and talents

Almost all parents want their children to be happy and successful in life. Parents therefore generally invest heavily in their children with financial and emotional resources. It grieves most fathers and mothers if they do not see their children grow into happy and successful adults despite this investment.

For sons and daughters to find success in life they need to use their gifts and talents (Ericsson et al, 1993). If, perhaps, for reasons of laziness or rebellion, they do not use these talents they frequently undermine not only their own success and happiness, but also that of their parents.

Children can also be negligent in expressions of gratitude to parents. Most parents, like children, like to know that they are loved and appreciated. Poor relationships with parents can often be improved with verbal declarations of appreciation and acts of practical kindness.

5.3 Correcting poor behaviour

Correcting poor fatherly behaviour

Addictive behaviours such as alcoholism and sexual compulsions are very damaging and are very important to correct. If fathers are plagued by strongly addictive behaviours, the evidence suggests that the best course of action is to seek professional help and to actively participate in a Twelve Step support group (CASA, 2001).

When a father seeks to correct some of his poor behaviour, it is important to realise that if he has not addressed issues with his own father and mother, it will be difficult to be a good parent himself. Addressing issues with parents is therefore of paramount importance. Chapter 6 discusses some of the ways this can be done.

> CASE STUDY: I (Robert) had a father who was absent from the home much of the time. The experience of longing for my father, of needing a primary male figure in my life in my first 20 years and the pain of not receiving it in my early years has been one of my greatest struggles. My desire and deep need for approval, validation, boundaries and initiation into manhood were not met. Some writers call this experience and journey the Father Hunger and Father Wound.
>
> There is an ancient saying, origins unknown, which suggests that -"What is not resolved is repeated". Richard Rohr has stated something very similar – "If the pain of your story is not transformed it will be transmitted".
>
> So what did I do when it came time to raise my own family? I repeated the historical patterns and pain of the past. I started a furniture manufacturing business in 1986 and over the years became extremely busy and stressed. The demands

of a growing business and a growing family was more than I knew how to balance, so my family suffered.

My fathering was accidental and dissipated. I was frequently physically absent from the home and when present, I was emotionally spent. In the late 1990s I had a wakeup call. I noticed that my children were growing up without me and I was missing out on them. I wasn't the father (or husband) I hoped to be.

It was time for change; I needed to modify my life direction, to grow up, to man up, to reject passivity, accept responsibility and live courageously – to become a better father, a better husband and a better man.

I began to read many books about parenting, manhood, fathering and all the associated material. I realised I needed to repair the wrongs of the past and I sought forgiveness for my failings.

I also started to reflect and have a time of quiet and stillness every morning. What began with 10 minutes is now today about 1 hour. This has helped me make the change process a journey, rather than a one-shot event.

Correcting poor behaviour on the part of sons or daughters

The issue of what sons and daughters can do to correct errant behaviour and attitudes towards fathers is a very important one and the next chapter is devoted to discussing it. While the topic is addressed in some detail in the next chapter, a brief case study on the issue is provided below.

CASE STUDY: When I (Peter) was a young adult I heard someone say that the way you treat your parents is the way you can expect your children to treat you. I felt very uncomfortable when I heard those words. I cringed at the thought that one day someone would treat me the way I had treated my parents.

When I was young I felt that parents should look after and care for their children selflessly and heroically. If they ever fell short of these lofty callings I was quick to judge. I had very different standards for myself. I felt that people should accept me the way I was. The hypocrisy of my attitudes was slow to dawn on me.

I am not sure if I am much less selfish or hypocritical now than when I was young. I do think, however, that I am shrewder now than when I was young. I have come to understand that each of us has a preferred language of love and our relationships improve most rapidly when we find the language of love of others and speak it.

In trying to improve my relationships with my parents, I found they responded much more strongly to certain kinds of behaviours than others. At one point I wrote a letter to my father and in the letter I said (among other things) that I loved him. It was not a big deal for me to say that but it seemed to be very important for my father. It seemed to be part of his language of love. Every week, then, for the last part of his life, I tried to remember to tell him that I loved him.

I found that my mother was very responsive to behaviours which showed her that her enormous investments in my life had borne at least some fruit. The fact that I became an engineer seemed to give her great joy. She came from a family of engineers and was proud of this heritage. She seemed to

> be delighted whenever I had successes in my career. I also found that my mother was deeply appreciative of small gifts that I gave her. Though the gifts were small, my mother was very grateful for them. Again, I think that the gifts were a sign to her that her investments were producing dividends, albeit very small ones.

5.4 Summary

- Very poor fathering appears to be worse than no fathering at all.
- Pornography is addictive and destructive to family relationships.
- Sexual abuse by a father tends to be less likely if the father is heavily involved in the care of the children in the early years and is living an ordered life with the mother.
- Sexual abuse is much more likely to be caused by a step-father than a biological father.
- Alcohol and drug dependencies are very destructive, especially because of the violence that they can foster.
- Emotional abuse is relatively common and tends to cause significant problems.
- Fathers can be heavily involved in their work and still be good fathers. The key is to involve the children in their professional lives.
- Excessive TV watching detracts from interactive time spent with family and sets a bad example for children.
- If children copy the example of fathers in watching too much TV, they run the risk of becoming obese.
- Good deceased fathers continue to cast a positive fatherly influence.
- To correct poor fathering, it is often necessary to deal with issues with one's own parents.

- Sons and daughters can contribute to bad relationships with fathers (and therefore to their own dysfunction) by being un-forgiving and judgmental towards fathers.
- Rebellion against appropriate fatherly discipline by sons and daughters also contributes to long-term dysfunction.
- If children fail to use their gifts and talents, they tend to undermine their future success and the hopes their parents have for them.

6

Turning the hearts of sons and daughters to parents

The evidence indicates that the quality of the relationship with the father has a very significant link to life outcomes (Allen and Daly, 2007; Vaillant, 2012). It is important to consider the implications of this finding – does it mean that those who did not grow up with a warm father-child relationship are doomed to unfulfilled, unhappy lives? The answer to this question is "No".

The Grant Study found that it was never too late to find happiness or to overcome difficulties. Other evidence indicates the same. Change is possible. The perceived warmth of the father-child relationship can be changed at any point in life via pro-active behaviour and attitude changes on the part of the son or daughter. Much change is possible, even in cases where the father has passed away. This chapter will discuss the various mechanisms which facilitate this kind of change, along with some supporting case studies.

6.1 The potential for restoration

When one is seeking to deal with an impoverished childhood, it is important to consider what level of restoration is possible. A study performed in 1996 provides some insights into this question.

CASE STUDY: In 1996 renowned academic, Mihaly Csikszentmihalyi, performed a ground-breaking study on creativity. In that study he investigated the background of over 90 people who had made an exceptional creative contribution to society (Csikszentmihalyi, 1996). These people included Nobel Prize winning scientists, eminent writers, medical pioneers, renowned composers, great architects and respected politicians. His investigations revealed that an unusually large number of these super-achievers had lost a father early in life.

The finding from this study is somewhat counter-intuitive. Many would have expected that people growing up without a father would be under-represented among super-achievers, not over-represented. The achievements of some fatherless men and women are, in fact, quite astounding. Isaac Newton lost his father while still in the womb and his mother then left him when he was just three years of age to live with her new husband. Isaac still managed to become arguably history's greatest ever scientist.

A key message from Csikszentmihalyi's study is that the absence of a biological father is not an insurmountable barrier to fulfilment in life. Many fatherless super-achievers found mentors to fill the gap left by their lost fathers. The loss of their fathers seems to have fostered a deep awareness of their need for nurture and in response, they developed an above average ability to source nurture from those around them.

CASE STUDY: Godfrey Minot Camille was one of the most memorable participants in the Grant Study of Adult Development (Vaillant, 2013). Camille's parents were wealthy but they had serious emotional problems. A psychiatrist engaged in the Grant Study classified Camille's childhood background as one of the bleakest in the group.

At university Camille was a hypochondriac. He regularly reported to the infirmary, but physical illnesses could rarely be found. Shortly after graduating as a doctor, he attempted suicide.

Camille hated having to deal with his patients because they always brought him their problems. He felt scarcely able to deal with his own problems, let alone help others.

To start to deal with some of his issues, he attended psychotherapy sessions and acquired a greater understanding of himself. He realised, for example, that his hypochondria had been a self-inflicted subconscious punishment for his aggressive desires.

At the age of 33 he had a major breakthrough. He was hospitalised for 14 months with pulmonary tuberculosis (TB) – a legitimate illness. He felt peace and security by being able to stay in bed for a year, able to do what he wanted and not have to answer to anyone. It was a reprieve from his traumatic life. He wrote during that period that he became convinced that "Someone with a capital 'S' cared about me". The experience was the first of several to cause dramatic changes in his life.

Afterwards Camille went through more psychotherapy, he returned to the church he had abandoned as a youth and he learned to love. By the end of the Grant Study, Camille was rated by the study's investigators as one of the happiest and

> most mature participants. At 75 he articulated the key to his restoration:
>
> "… only love can make us real. Denied this in my boyhood for reasons I now understand, it took me years to tap substitute sources. What seems marvellous is how many there are and how restorative they prove. What durable and pliable creatures we are, and what a storehouse of goodness lurks in the social fabric. … I never dreamed my later years would be so stimulating and rewarding".
>
> Despite his shaky start, Camille was able to radically turn his life around. It took substantial time, but he started to love helping his patients and he learned to love and be loved through his family and others around him. A psychiatrist from the Grant Study interviewed his daughter towards the end of Camille's life and she gave the most convincing proclamation of daughter-father love of any of the children the psychiatrist interviewed (Vaillant, 2013).

The findings from the Grant Study and the Csikszentmihalyi Study are consistent. It is possible to more than recover from an impoverished childhood. With the right attitudes it is actually possible to turn the experience into an advantage.

6.2 Starting the journey of restoration and healing – identifying the root causes

To be able to start the process of restoration and healing, one has to move on from the debilitating events of the past. Forgiveness and gratitude are important parts of this process. A lack of forgiveness is detrimental to physical, emotional and mental health (Linden and Maercker, 2011;

Worthington, E, 2004). Similarly, habitual ingratitude can engulf a person in a very destructive negativity.

While un-forgiveness and other wrong attitudes are detrimental at any stage of life, they are particularly problematical in the critical period between conception and six years of age. These early years of life constitute the training phase of the human brain. For this reason, patterns of thinking and behaviour learned and practised during those years tend to be replicated over and over again throughout life. To repair broken lives, then, one has to pay particular attention to the early years.

The need to undo the wrongs of these early years presents a dilemma. Most people do not remember what transpired in the early years. The solution to this problem is to recognise that if patterns of un-forgiveness and dysfunctional behaviour are established in the early years, those patterns tend to repeatedly manifest in an observable way throughout life. Engaging with unhealthy mental and behavioural practices before the age of six is analogous to building a defective factory which continually produces poor quality goods.

The structures in these 'thought factories' can be deduced by the patterns of poor thinking and behaviour they produce. These defective patterns eventually tend to produce unpleasant circumstances or suffering, and it is this suffering which provides motivational opportunities for serious reflection and remedial action.

Of course, not all reflection leads people to a correct diagnosis of the problem, or to correct remedial action. Sometimes, an unwillingness to face reality can lead a person to even more damaging behaviour. It might be, for example, that some people find themselves beset by poverty as a just consequence of their errant behaviour and attitudes. Reflection might prompt them to think that the solution is to steal or cheat. This might provide a temporary respite, but will lead to greater problems in the long-term. If such people wish to recover fully, their reflections need to be brave. Thorny issues will almost certainly need to be faced at some point.

If corrupt patterns of thinking and behaving are not arrested there is a strong possibility they will be passed from generation to generation. This is so because children copy the example of their parents, especially in the early years. The situation is analogous to planting a bad seed which grows into a bad tree which spawns more bad seeds. With this kind of spreading mechanism many can be badly affected, not just children, but grandchildren, great grandchildren and even others in a community or nation.

Because of this trans-generational propagation effect it is frequently necessary to look for troublesome patterns in family trees. It is even sometimes necessary to look at recurring patterns in nations and ethnic groups.

> CASE STUDY: For much of my life I (Peter) had a very strong sense of rejection which severely limited me in in my ability to take risks. One day I was thinking about my predicament and tried working backwards from the effect to see if I could identify the cause.
>
> Because of the intensity of the effect I felt the cause had to be rooted in the formative years – mine or possibly someone else's. It seemed to me that the only event that could generate the kind of feelings and experiences I was having was the abandonment of a young child.
>
> After thinking about these issues I went to talk with one of my parents. I told them (perhaps impetuously) that I was convinced that someone in our family had abandoned a baby. I don't know what I was expecting to hear in response, but what I did hear amazed me. I was told that I was right. My grandfather had been abandoned by his parents as an infant. This abandonment was something I had never heard about before.

> My great grandparents were moving from Europe to Australia and they felt that the journey to Australia would be too dangerous for a baby. They had therefore left the baby with his grandparents until he was eight years old. I was told that my grandfather resented being left in Europe until the day he died.
>
> The un-forgiveness of my grandfather had probably festered and propagated across the generations. Sadly, it found a ready and willing receptacle in me. After discovering this root cause I had to deal with it. The first step was to let go of the un-forgiveness that I had given into from an early age. The second step was to commit to a journey of behavioural change and restoration, the kind of journey that is described below.

6.3 The journey of behavioural change and restoration

It is important to ask whether or not turning away from un-forgiveness and other wrong attitudes is sufficient to fully eliminate negative consequences in our lives. In answering this question it is pertinent to consider an analogous question. If alcoholics who were driven to alcoholism by unresolved anger manage to resolve their anger, will their problems disappear? The answer is no, not usually. Resolving the anger sets these people on the right path, but it does not in itself alleviate all their problems. Rather it provides a heightened opportunity for them on the road to wholeness. They will probably still need to go through a Twelve Step type program to achieve full restoration.

It is similar with those who have broken lives due to issues of childhood deprivation. Mental and behavioural habit patterns tend to be entrenched and there is an addictive element to these habit patterns. To overcome this addictive power, the spirit undergirding the Twelve Step program typically needs to be embraced.

6.4 A Twelve Step approach to restoration

The Twelve Step process presented below is derived directly from the one pioneered by the founders of Alcoholics Anonymous. The process below really only differs from the original one in that it addresses recovery from behavioural and mental addictions rather that physical addictions.

Step 1: We admitted that we ourselves [alone] are helpless to overcome our problems.

Step 2: We acknowledged that we need a higher power.

The reliance on a higher power is one of the issues in Twelve Step Programs which attracts much attention. Many people want to achieve restoration but do not believe in God. Generally, Twelve Step programs do not insist that members believe in God and there are many members who do not. Some, for example, believe simply in the combined strength of the support group as the higher power to assist them in their restoration. At the same time it is informative to look at the evidence on whether belief in God affects recovery rates. That evidence is considered in Chapter 9.

Step 3: We made a decision to turn our will and our lives over to the care of God as *we understood him.*

Step 4: We made a searching and moral inventory of ourselves.

> CASE STUDY: During my life I (Peter) periodically had financial struggles and these struggles often provoked me to resentment and stress. The aggravation eventually led me to start trying to find the roots of my problem.
>
> I concluded from the patterns occurring in my life that I

> had some un-forgiveness towards my parents in the area of financial provision. My parents had been poor but hard working people, and for the most part, I really appreciated their efforts. Part of the young child in me, however, had given in to resentment because they did not give me everything that I wanted.
>
> I realised that I had to change my attitude. I also started looking for 'substitute sources' of financial provision. I didn't know how to find these kinds of sources myself, so I just asked God if he would be prepared to find them for me.
>
> Shortly afterwards, an unusual sequence of events occurred. I had organised to go on a brief holiday to New Zealand, but the person with whom I was planning to go pulled out. Because I still wanted to go, I contacted a group in New Zealand who I thought might have some people planning a trip. The group told me that there were some people doing a tour of the South Island and that I was welcome to join them.
>
> I was happy to hear this and booked my fare. When I arrived in New Zealand and started travelling with these people, the group leader welcomed me very warmly. He told me that they already had enough money to cover the whole tour around the South Island, so I did not need to give them anything. He told me that all my accommodation, internal airfares, food and activities would be covered. He told me to just consider it a gift from God.

Step 5: We admitted to God, to ourselves and to another human being the exact nature of our wrongs.

Note that people often need someone else to whom they can not only admit their wrongs, but who can also help to objectively identify the root causes of problems. Wise and enlightened counsellors, from a support group or elsewhere, can help in this regard. There may be some people who are in need of counselling and who do not know where to look. For these people we have gathered information on some suggested contacts and listed them in Appendix III.

> CASE STUDY: In 1983 a little boy was born in a Queensland hospital and this tiny child was given up for adoption by his biological parents.
>
> One loving Queensland couple had a strong yearning to have and care for children, but were unable to conceive. They therefore decided to pursue adoption. They were delighted to be able to arrange with an adoption agency to bring the little boy home and care for him.
>
> One day when the boy was about six years old the adoptive father and son went to find a dog and bring him home as a pet. After they had selected a pet the little boy's eyes welled up with tears. He asked what was going to happen to the dogs that got left behind.
>
> The father immediately recognised what was going on in the boy's mind. He gently asked the boy if he was worried about his Mom and Dad leaving him behind at the hospital. The little boy said "Yes".
>
> The father then asked his son if he would be prepared to forgive his Mom and Dad and the little boy said "Yes". He then asked his son if he would let him pray for him and for his Mom and Dad. Again, the little boy said "Yes".
>
> This response by the child (and the father) had a powerful effect on the boy's life. Much of the sting was taken out of his sense of rejection. He 'moved on' and was empowered to

> drink in the love that his adoptive mother and father lavished on him.
>
> The little boy grew to not only be able to receive love but also to give it. As he aged he was able to regularly tell his father and mother that he loved them. He also went on to care for a family of his own.

Step 6: We were entirely ready to have God remove all these defects of character.

Step 7: We humbly asked Him to remove our shortcomings.

It is advisable to engage with Steps 3-7 repeatedly until all the dysfunctional thinking and behavioural patterns disappear. This is necessary for a number of reasons. Firstly, flawed mental processes are normally firmly ingrained. They will often not shift without determined effort. Secondly, the problems encountered in life are often over-determined. That is, they have multiple root causes. We need to persevere until *all* the problems are identified and dealt with. While some level of improvement may come quickly, full recovery may take a substantial period of time.

A case study below is offered to provide some context for Steps 3-7.

> CASE STUDY: Throughout the early part of my life I (Peter) had major difficulties at work. These difficulties were quite stressful for me, as I spent a lot of my conscious hours at work. In the process of trying to resolve my work problems I found not one, but three different root causes.
>
> One of the consistent patterns I experienced at work was difficult relationships with my bosses. In some cases I had bosses who were demanding and unreasonable. In other cases,

though, I actually had likeable bosses, but remarkably, I still found myself relating to them as if they were unreasonable. I realised that a dysfunctional pattern of expectation must have been set up in my childhood. I concluded that from an early age I must have refused to forgive one of my parents for being (in my childhood estimation) overly demanding. I knew I had to forgive and change my attitude. When I did that, things improved, but my troubles at work did not completely disappear.

I kept searching for other root causes. One day I came to an important realisation. I had made a decision early in life that I was going to take the easy path through life. I would avoid things that were hard.

As a result of my decision to take things easy, it seemed that I attracted hard task masters who would regularly try and push me out of my comfort zone. I really did not want any more hard task masters, so I resolved to voluntarily try and start extending myself more fully.

Finally, I had a third conviction about the cause of my work-place difficulties. Part of my family was of Irish descent. Throughout their history the Irish experienced much suffering in their work lives, which they attributed to overly demanding English masters. As a result, I suspect, they developed habit patterns of un-forgiveness.

As I looked at my family tree I could see many family members who were experiencing similar patterns of work problems to me. I became convinced that there was a serious generational effect plaguing my family. Clearly, it seemed to me, there were others in my family needing help as well.

In summary, I found three different root causes for the

> major ongoing problems I experienced in my work. It was after dealing with all three root causes that I started to find great fulfilment in my work.

Step 8: We made a list of all persons we had harmed and became willing to make amends to them all.

Step 9: We made direct amends to such people wherever possible, except when to do so would injure them or others.

If child-parent relationships have broken down there is probably some fault on the part of the child and some on the part of the parent. Children should take responsibility for their part in the breakdown. Thus the child usually needs to try to reach out in some way to achieve at least a measure of reconciliation. The advice of wise counsellors can assist in knowing when and how this can be achieved.

Step 10: We continued to take personal inventory and when we were wrong promptly admitted it.

As suggested above, ongoing problems typically have multiple root causes and taking a moral inventory of wrongdoing needs to be done on multiple occasions to identify these root causes. The following paragraphs give some examples of commonly encountered root causes.

A wrong that is frequently committed is to habitually choose that which gains us approval rather than that which is right. This type of habit pattern often starts if a child judges (rightly or wrongly) that their parent(s) will only love and accept them if they behave in certain ways. If a child gives in to this kind of dysfunctional thinking they may develop an 'approval addiction'. They will regularly live out their life to gain the acceptance and approval of others and happiness will elude them. They will often experience much anger and frustration in life.

A second wrong that is often committed by children is to disrespect their parent(s). If for example, a child has a parent who does not firmly enforce discipline, that child may disregard the parent's instructions and additionally disrespect the parent. This can lead to a habit pattern of disregarding and/or disrespecting authority figures generally. Often, such a person will receive inadequate guidance and will not have a properly formed character. They will typically develop some measure of incompetence as a result.

An alternative path to disrespecting parents may occur if a child has a parent whom the child judges to be overly harsh. That child may respond by harbouring resentment towards the parent and eventually towards authority figures in general.

Yet another common form of wrongdoing finds its fulfilment in sexual promiscuity. If a child has had very little affection from their father or mother or both, they may try to seek this affection through sexual relationships. Young women may engage in early sexual activity in an effort to tap into the emotional nurture they sought, but did not receive, from their father. As discussed in Chapter 1, young women from early father-absent families have teen pregnancy rates which are seven to eight times the rate for young women from intact two parent families (Ellis et al, 2003; Jeynes, 2001).

Step 11: We sought through prayer and meditation to improve our conscious contact with God *as we understood him*, praying only for knowledge of his will for us and the power to carry that out.

Step 12: Having had a spiritual awakening as the result of these steps, we tried to carry this message to others with similar problems, and to practise these principles in all our affairs.

CASE STUDY: Because of the growing awareness of the consequences of fatherlessness, many support groups and initiatives are appearing throughout the world.

One such group is Long Island Youth Mentoring program in the United States. This is a group which calls males of fatherly age to spend two to five hours a week mentoring fatherless children. The group essentially asks people to respond to the call to be a father for those without fathers. The group uses the mentoring approach because it has been found to be comparatively successful.

Studies have shown that mentoring:

i) reduces drug abuse by 46%,
ii) curbs violent behaviour by 52%,
iii) reduces teen pregnancy by 35%,
iv) cuts school drop-outs by 52%.

(http://www.liyouthmentoring.com/mentor-a-child/why-mentoring-matters/)

These types of programs not only help fatherless children, but they also provide an avenue for people to consolidate their own restoration by reaching out to others. That is, these programs provide a way for people to live out the final step of the Twelve Step program.

CASE STUDY: As I (Robert) have discussed earlier in this book, I struggled with my childhood relationship with my father and with the fathering of my own children. As I started to confront important issues, I began sharing my experiences with some trusted men. In the process I discovered that all of them struggled with the same issues. All of them were searching for integrity, intentionality and authenticity just as I was. I thought I was the only person in the world struggling with these issues and problems. I was wrong.

I found that most men who were prepared to be vulnerable expressed similar wounding and pain. So in 2003, along with a few brave men, I started an outreach to men called *menALIVE*. Since then we have worked with men in every state in Australia and New Zealand.

During the past 10 years we have come to the realisation that the overwhelming majority of men have father wounds due to absent fathering. Some men have been seriously damaged by not only absent fathers but by fathers that were present but angry, abusive and driven by addictions. There have been men who never knew their biological fathers, either because their fathers passed away early in their life or because the fathers left. *menALIVE* has sought to be a community of substitute sources of nurture for these men. It has also sought to encourage men to rise to their calling to be good fathers and leaders in their communities.

The response to *menALIVE* in Australia and New Zealand is testimony to the significance of the father wounding problem and the need for restoration. As of July, 2014, about 12,500 men had participated in one or more *menALIVE* events.

6.5 Adjustment of beliefs and thinking processes

Wrong responses in childhood often dispose a person to adopting harmful beliefs and thinking processes which persist later in life. These beliefs and thinking processes need to be changed in order for a person to attain happiness and success as an adult. The most suitable environment for facilitating the necessary changes is an environment of love. This is so because oxytocin and/or vasopressin tend to be released when a person experiences a very strong sense of love and these chemicals facilitate a dramatic and lasting rewiring of neural connections in the brain. Changes in beliefs and thinking are therefore likely to be easier and longer lasting if they are pursued within a loving milieu.

One of the best known formalised methodologies for adjusting beliefs and thinking processes is Cognitive Behaviour Therapy (CBT) (Hassett et al, 2009). The rationale behind CBT is that changes in one domain of the human person can affect other domains. Maladaptive beliefs and thinking can lead to changes in behaviour and feelings. Changes in behaviour can also lead to changes in thinking and emotions. Conventional CBT focuses heavily on changing thinking processes and behaviours, an approach which has been shown to be effective in various areas of human dysfunction (Dressen et al, 2010; Matusiewicz et al, 2010; Otte, 2001). CBT has six distinct phases (Gatchel et al, 2008):

i) Assessment of the problem.
ii) Reconceptualization (or cognitive adjustment).
iii) Acquisition of skills.
iv) Consolidation of skills and application training.
v) Generalization and maintenance.
vi) Post-treatment assessment and follow-up.

The counsellor or computer program facilitating CBT will typically try to challenge a person's maladaptive beliefs, thinking processes and behaviours, in an attempt to move them towards more constructive and adaptive ones. This challenge is often provided in the context of trying to achieve some long-term goal. Typical flaws in thinking that are targeted are:

i) exaggerating negatives,
ii) downplaying positives,
iii) overgeneralising and
iv) catastrophising.

Because the human mind is resistant to sudden changes in beliefs and attitudes, it is best if challenges are provided at spaced intervals and in an ongoing way. While some people are proficient at reflecting on and challenging their own beliefs and thinking processes, many are not. Many people need counsellors to guide them.

> CASE STUDY: Robyn was a woman who felt that her life was falling apart. She had just separated from her husband, her youngest child had left home to go to university, she had been through a stressful time at work following a restructure and she had been diagnosed by her doctor with depression. She was worried about losing her job, was anxious about everything and could not relax.
>
> Robyn's doctor suggested that a CBT approach might help her to cope better. She took her doctor's advice and went to a counsellor trained in the use of CBT. The counsellor suggested that they map out a program, meet for eight sessions, and then review progress.
>
> Together, Robyn and her counsellor tried to document the thinking, behaviour, feelings and physical state associated with her anxiety. Their summary of the situation is given below.

Thinking

She thought she was old and unattractive.

She thought she was not coping.

She thought she would lose her job.

She thought she would find it very difficult if she lost her job.

She thought her friends were bored with her.

She thought that even her son was glad to be escaping from her.

Feelings

She felt lonely.

She felt sad.

She felt irritable.

She felt resentful.

She felt let down.

She felt angry.

She felt anxious.

She felt guilty.

Behaviour

She stayed at home much of the time.

She wrote angry letters to her ex-husband.

She stopped exercising.

She started eating junk food.

She started drinking more than usual.

She became impatient with her mother.

Physical state

She started having problems sleeping.

She started putting on weight.

She had headache problems and an upset stomach.

She was jumpy and restless.

She was very fatigued.

Robyn's counsellor believed that the best way to move forward was to begin with her behaviour, and then progress on to her thinking processes. In her various meetings with her counsellor Robyn agreed to:

i) start going out more regularly with friends,
ii) cook some healthy meals for herself,
iii) occasionally invite people over to share a meal with her,
iv) do some regular bike riding and
v) keep a written record of her negative thoughts and how she responded to them.

Robyn was also encouraged to consider her negative beliefs and weigh up the evidence for the validity of those beliefs. She was then encouraged to think about alternative ways of thinking about her circumstances which were more objective and constructive.

At the end of her eight sessions Robyn was happy to find herself feeling much better. She was now doing regular exercise, she was socialising more, she was sleeping more

> soundly and she was experiencing less anxiety and bitterness. The behavioural and cognitive changes seemed to have provoked changes in the emotional and physical domain, as hoped.
>
> (The above case study is a composite of the experiences of several patients, and is adapted from http://www.cbtoxford.com/cbt-oxford/10-case-studies/14-depression-with-anxiety).

CBT is just one of a number of therapies which have proven helpful in the restoration of broken lives. Family Therapy is another (Stratton, 2005). A full discussion on the various helpful therapies available is beyond the scope of this book.

6.6 Summary

- It is quite possible to turn an impoverished family background into an advantage.
- To overcome the effects of a poor relationship with one or more parents, one needs a deep hunger for connection and restoration.
- To commence the journey of restoration one has to forgive parents and significant others.
- To identify areas of un-forgiveness we cannot rely on feelings. A better way is to identify which areas of life are going badly. There is a strong possibility of un-forgiveness towards, or judgment of, a parent in those areas.
- Un-forgiveness and other wrong tendencies often propagate across the generations.

- The journey of restoration can be expedited by adopting a Twelve Step approach.
- A key part of restoration involves reaching out to help others with similar problems.
- Beliefs and attitudes must be changed during the restoration process and CBT can be useful for affecting such changes.

7

Turning the hearts of parents to sons and daughters

7.1 Parental initiative

It is not always the son or daughter who initiates improvements to parent-child relationships. Sometimes it is the parent. Moreover, it is not only biological parents (important as they are) who can enrich the lives of children. Substitute parents and other role models can make a major impression on the lives of children as well (King, 2006; Neuman, 2010; Yuan and Hamilton, 2006).

> CASE STUDY: Roman Pazniewski was a man who found it easy to tell his wife that he loved her, but not his daughters.
>
> On one week-end event he heard a talk about the importance of telling cherished ones that they are loved. After that talk he decided to tell his daughters that they were beautiful, that he loved them and was proud of them.
>
> His description of what happened after that is given below in his own words:

My adopted daughter spent the first months of her life in hospital. No mother, father or close relatives to hold and hug her and tell her she is loved and precious. I am told that if a child doesn't bond with someone in the first months of life, they probably never will for the rest of their life. That certainly seemed to be true with Nati. She did not want to be hugged, held or touched. She kept me at arms length … for sixteen years. I compounded the problem by being critical of her behaviour and pointing out her many misdemeanours.

After that weekend talk about telling dear ones they are loved, I decided that I would tell my daughters that they were beautiful and that I loved them and was proud of them…. and I did, as soon as I came home. You can just imagine the response I got from my two teenage daughters.

"Mum, what's wrong with Dad??" – and, "Mum, what is Dad taking?'"

I wasn't discouraged and continued every day to tell them that I loved them and that they were pretty, that they were beautiful and special.

After 15 weeks, Nati felt comfortable enough to give me a tiny hug. I wept with joy! Now, I get a hug *every day!*

Roman Pazniewski

CASE STUDY: Sheneau Stanley is a man who understands the importance of relationships with parents. He also knows that forgiveness is one of the fastest ways to improve those relationships. Aware of these facts, he sometimes speaks to people and says:

"I'm going to stand in the place of your father and go through a list of questions and ask you for forgiveness on behalf of your fathers."

He knows that many of their biological fathers will never do this; and so he steps in as a substitute father. He then works through a list of questions, one after the other, with a pause in between, allowing them time to respond. The questions might be, say:

Will you forgive me for putting a word curse on you by saying that you were stupid or fat?

Will you forgive me for not spending enough time with you?

Will you forgive me for not telling you that I loved you?

Will you forgive me for not playing with you when you were young?

Will you forgive me for not affirming your masculinity/femininity?

> Will you forgive me for not trying to understand you?
>
> As he goes through the list, the people can nod yes or no if the question stirs something in them. For some it is a very healing exercise. It allows them to get in touch with hurts and provides them with an opportunity to forgive and to move on with their lives.
>
> The same type of exercise could, of course, be used for addressing un-forgiveness towards mothers, but the exercise would probably best be conducted by a motherly figure rather than a fatherly one.

Using the workplace to improve parent child relationships

Bruce Robinson is a Western Australian doctor who performed an investigation into the effect of busy careers on fatherhood. He interviewed over 75 fathers in busy jobs, including former Australian Prime Minister, John Howard. One of the key findings from his work was somewhat counter-intuitive. Robinson's investigation found that it was quite common for men with busy and demanding jobs to be successful fathers. In fact, fathers with successful careers often tended to be more effective than fathers with less successful careers.

Many busy men achieved their success as fathers by involving their children in their work (Robinson, 2001). Some of these men, for example, took their children with them on conference trips or they involved them in their political campaigns or they made them part of the family business.

7.2 Relationships and trauma

The chemical releases that occur when compassion or assistance is dispensed after trauma seem to facilitate a similar kind of bonding to that which occurs when parents beget children or when people fall in love. This effect is so powerful that it can even cause hostages to bond with their captors if the hostages discover that their lives are going to be spared. This phenomenon is known as the Stockholm Syndrome and has been found to occur in about 27% of hostage situations (Fuselier, 1999).

One implication of this trauma-bonding effect is that fathers (both natural and substitute ones) can actually wield great power if they wisely take the initiative after trauma in their children's lives.

> CASE STUDY: Reuven Feuerstein was born in Botosami, Romania, in 1921. In 1944 he fled the Nazi persecution and found his way to Jerusalem. While there he started working with children who had lost their parents in the holocaust. During IQ testing, Feuerstein found that many of these children had severely retarded cognitive functioning, often performing between three to six years below average for their ages.
>
> Feuerstein was moved with fatherly compassion for these children and refused to accept the conventional wisdom that they could not change their IQs. He spent many hours working with them and researching cognitive and pedagogical strategies that could help them to learn. He devised practical exercises that would stretch them in the cognitive domain. He also taught them thinking and reflection strategies.
>
> Feuerstein's fatherly intervention had an enormous effect on the children. Many of them started to function at normal levels and were eventually able to attend regular schools.
>
> In 1948 Feuerstein was diagnosed with TB and went to Switzerland to recover. While there he studied Psychology at

the University of Geneva under Carl Jung and Jean Piaget. He returned to Israel in 1955 and resumed working with young survivors of trauma. During this time he decided to dedicate his life's work to them and in the process, created the International Center for the Enhancement of Learning Potential (ICELP).

One of the boys who had attended Feuerstein's center was a young man named Daniel. He suffered massive brain damage and fell into a vegetative state after a swimming accident. His parents were told by a leading medical specialist in France that the boy's condition was irreversible and that he would remain in a vegetative state all of his life.

Daniel's parents subsequently heard about Feuerstein's center in Jerusalem and took their son there to be treated. The results of this treatment were astonishing. Eventually, Daniel started speaking again, he started being able to care for himself alone and he even enrolled in a course at the Hebrew University (Neuman, 2010).

Feuerstein claims that if one is going to make a difference to children's lives, one has to invest in them, devoting large amounts of time and careful attention to them.

Feuerstein has effectively fathered many traumatised children to maturity, including some with Down Syndrome. His own grandson, Elhanan, was born with Down Syndrome, and Feuerstein and his son, Ravi, worked on intensively fathering the boy from birth. Now the child has matriculated from high school and has thus far lived an apparently fulfilling life.

Feuerstein's life and work reveals that fatherly intervention can make a huge difference not just to the cognitive elite, but even to those at the very margins of society.

7.3 The process of restoration

The story of Reuven Feuerstein illustrates many of the key principles of effective parental initiative. Biological parents (and to some extent grandparents and other relatives) are the most natural candidates for parental intervention, particularly in the early years of life. This is due in no small part to the bonding that is set up then with the release of powerful chemicals such as oxytocin and vasopressin. If these biological parents and relatives spend significant amounts of time with their children in the early years, the bonds of love and trust are powerfully reinforced.

Reuven and his son, Ravi, intervened intensively in the life of Elhanan, their grandson and son, respectively. Not surprisingly, then, the boy was able to develop well above average achievement levels for a Down Syndrome child.

Feuerstein also showed that it is possible for non-biological fathers to successfully intervene in the lives of children as a type of substitute father. In doing so, he followed many of the Twelve Step principles. That is, he began with an acknowledgement that neither he nor the children could achieve restoration with their own resources alone. He believed that he needed a higher power and regularly sought advice from Rabbi Menachem Mendel Schneerson.

Feuerstein also took regular moral inventory, reflected often, studied hard and even exploited the trauma-bonding effect. Additionally he committed to helping others to re-father children. He achieved this by giving many seminars, by producing numerous inspirational training documents and by creating his acclaimed center in Jerusalem.

> CASE STUDY: I (Peter) once worked with a woman who struck me as being unusually happy and well balanced. One day I asked her if she had a good relationship with her

father. She told me she had a fantastic father and a fantastic relationship with him. She said that she found it easy to relate to men and she had a good relationship with her husband and brothers as well. Her father, it seemed, had a positive influence not only on her, but on everyone in her family. According to the woman, her husband had even learned his parenting skills from his father in law.

It was obvious to me that this woman had a lot to contribute. On one occasion I asked her if she would be interested in coming to our church sometime. I said that the church needed people like her. (She had grown up in the same denomination as I had, but did not go regularly at that time). She told me that the church was too far away from where she lived and so she would decline. I thought she may have felt awkward about my inviting her and so I decided I would not bring up the subject any more. She, however, brought up the issue with me.

It was several months later at an end of year work event and she started telling me how grateful she was for my invitation and encouragement. I was very surprised. Her response helped me to appreciate that people need to know that they have something to contribute and that their contribution will be valued.

Everyone has something to offer by way of intervention in a broken life and there is a double reward when a person does offer their gifts and service. Rewards flow to the giver and receiver. It is good to consider how we can contribute. Do we have gifts in hospitality? Do we have skills in working with emotionally broken people? Do we have the ability to empathise with and encourage others? Do we have skills in writing? Do we have the ability to challenge others without offending them? Do we have musical or other creative gifts? Do we have practical or other skills?

7.3 The benefits of parental initiative for parents

This book has argued for for parents (and fathers in particular) to reclaim their vitally important place as conduits of love in the lives of their children. Mothers almost always try to be heavily involved in their children's lives – fathers, less so, on average. If fathers do become strongly involved they are likely to help not only their children, but also themselves.

According to the research, involved fathers tend to have fewer premature deaths, they tend to be engaged in less substance abuse, they tend to get into less trouble with the law and they tend to have a stronger sense of well-being (Pleck, 1997).

> CASE STUDY: Mike de Boer had a very troubled life. His parents divorced shortly after he was born and he stated in 2011 that he had seen his father only twice since then.
>
> For most of his life Mike lived a dangerous and destructive existence. He was addicted to drugs and spent two terms in prison. He spent time in 'rehab' and had the encouragement of a parole officer who tried to help him kick the drug habit. His prison terms, his rehab and his parole officer, however, were not able to make him give up drugs. What eventually convinced him to turn his life around was the birth of a little red headed boy, his son.
>
> Mike summed up how his son's life had changed him:
>
> "There is nothing in this world that is going to keep me from being there for my little man".

CASE STUDY: James Hetfield is the lead singer of Metallica. His father left him and moved out of the family home when he was 13 years of age. He spoke about his experiences in an interview during the documentary called, *Absent*. He said that

"There is a father wound that you never recover from. ... I was never taught to step up and become a man".

The birth of his son, however, gave him new determination to move beyond his problems. Despite his own pain he resolved that:

"the lineage of that [father wound] stops here ... I'm doing the best to become the best father I can be right now for my children".

CASE STUDY: "My son, you're a Dad". "Congratulations Robert".

My father, John, enthusiastically spoke these words like a blessing over me on April 17, 1987. It was on the morning of Good Friday that my first child was born. What a profound moment in my life, not just because it was a painfully traumatic experience, especially for my wife Alicia as the big baby was pulled into the world by high forceps delivery, but also at the same time it was triumphantly terrific. "It's a boy!" A son was born.

The whole experience was surprisingly exceptional, like this

> was the beginning of something momentous and hopefully magnificent. It was a significant and prominent transition in my journey as a man. In that instant I was changed. I became a father. I had arrived too!
>
> Incapable of containing the tears, joy and relief I looked at my son. I saw him, touched him, held him, smelled him and kissed him, marvelling at the miracle and revelling in the mystery of the moment. Look what I made! So many feelings and sensations were swirling in those minutes. From somewhere deep, a new place deep within me was revealed; a strange surge of tactile, tangible warmth, a form of love I had never experienced before.

7.5 Summary

- Both biological and substitute parents can initiate repair of the damage done by broken parent-child relationships.
- Fathers can be successful in both careers and family if they involve their children in their work.
- Parental intervention in situations of great trauma (by natural and substitute parents) can be particularly powerful.
- To sustain efforts at restoration, the principles underpinning the Twelve Step program are useful.
- To 'move on' sons and daughters need to forgive their parents. Interventions by parents (natural or substitute) which foster forgiveness can therefore be quite helpful.
- All adults have the ability to contribute in some way to the restoration of broken lives in the community around them.

- Fathers who involve themselves in their children's lives have i) fewer premature deaths, ii) less substance abuse, iii) less trouble with the law and iv) a greater sense of well-being.

8

Turning the hearts of fathers to mothers and mothers to fathers

A father who responsibly cares for his children is of significant benefit to the children's mother. He helps the mother by lessening the parental load on her and by contributing to the formation of more whole and happy children. The co-parent relationship has a very strong impact on the parenting ability of both mothers and fathers.

Mothers who experience relationship problems with their children's fathers tend to be more emotionally spent and more irritable. They tend to be less emotionally positive in dealing with children and exercise harsher and more erratic discipline. They also tend to respond to their children in less patient and less nurturing ways (Amato, 1998).

Research also shows that mothers who have supportive husbands tend to have more trouble-free pregnancies, less post-partem depression and better nursing experiences (Biller, 1993).

The relationships between the father and the mother and between the parents and child are all important for the child's future (Marsiglio et al, 2000). In the case of a non-resident father the provision of child support (which assists both the mother and the child) has been found to help the child's academic progress, nutrition and health. Child support has also been found to correlate negatively with behaviour problems (Amato and Gilreth, 1999; Argys et al, 1998; Graham et al, 1994).

A mother can assist the father to be a good parent by welcoming and encouraging the father's involvement with the children. While many mothers do actively welcome this involvement, a significant number do not. Some mothers doubt the fathers' competence, are unwilling to compromise on their standards for housekeeping or child rearing and fear losing influence with their children. These attitudes significantly undermine a father's performance in his role (Allen and Hawkins, 1999).

8.1 The co-parenting environment

A good deal of evidence indicates that men function more effectively as fathers when they are in stable and loving marriages (Bouchard and Lee, 2000; Furstenberg and Cherlin, 1991).

Fathering and marriage tend to be strongly linked in the minds of many men. They tend to see the marriage environment and childrearing as a 'package deal' (Townsend, 2002). Sadly, then, when marriages fail the involvement of many fathers deteriorates substantially.

It is not only a stable marriage structure which is important. The quality of the marital relationship has great relevance as well. Unresolved conflict between parents within a marriage has been found to associate negatively with the child's academic development, behaviour, self-esteem and social skills (Amato, 1998; Cummings and O'Reilly, 1998; Davies and Cummings, 1994).

Importantly, fatherly involvement also enhances marital harmony and success. Researchers have found that involvement in fathering accounts for about 25% of midlife marital success (Snarey, 1993).

Why cooperative parenting matters

When parents cooperate and agree on decisions and boundaries, children are more likely to see parental authority in a legitimate light, rather than as something random or arbitrary. Cooperative parenting also provides good modelling for children. It is very helpful for children to see their parents communicating well, showing one another respect and resolving conflicts with negotiation and compromise. These behaviours can then be internalised and used by the children in their dealings with their peers and with partners later in life (Amato, 2005).

Observing conflict between parents, on the other hand, induces stress in children. If this stress manifests during the early years, it is particularly problematical; the children may not have the emotional resources to cope.

Conflict between parents can be particularly damaging when children feel they are 'caught in the middle'. Children can be provoked to feel this way if:

i) one parent speaks negatively about the other parent in front of the children,
ii) children are recruited by one parent as allies against the other parent or
iii) children are asked to convey hurtful messages from one parent to the other.

If children do feel that they are caught in the middle it tends to reduce their sense of attachment to one or both parents.

Conflict between the mother and the father

All relationships have some degree of conflict, but some conflicts are particularly potent and damaging. Those conflicts which tend to affect us most are often the ones that touch on raw nerves from childhood and which involve flawed early responses to parents.

> CASE STUDY: One woman found early in her marriage that she was becoming very resentful of the amount of time her husband was spending at his work.
>
> As she tried to work through her issues she had a flashback to her childhood. She was sitting under a tree asking herself "Why doesn't my father take us to the beach?" It was a Saturday and from the little girl's perspective, it was an ideal time to go to the beach. Her father, however, worked on Saturdays.
>
> The woman then realised that her resentment was part of a repeating life pattern – one in which she judged the significant male in her life for spending too much time at work.
>
> She realised that if she did not break this pattern her quality of life would deteriorate. She made a choice to forgive her father and adopt a new and more positive attitude towards her husband. She started cherishing the time that she did spend with him instead of being bitter about the time she did not spend with him.
>
> The husband, for his part, had grown up with a mother who had a tendency to be critical. As he expended significant energy on his work he encountered resentment from the significant woman in his life. He also realised that there was a repeating pattern. He decided to forgive his mother and change his attitude to his wife.
>
> Because the man and woman were both prepared to face their un-resolved issues with their parents, they were able to avoid major ongoing tension in their marriage.

In dealing with major conflicts it is important to ask ourselves the question. "Has this kind of thing happened before in my life and if so, where?" We may well find that the conflict is part of an ongoing pattern which started in childhood. If so, we need to forego anger towards those who first hurt us.

8.2 Summary

- If fathers are unsupportive, mothers tend to be more emotionally stretched, less consistent with their discipline, less patient and less nurturing with their children.
- If a mother is unsupportive of the father's involvement, the father tends to be less effective as a parent.
- Fathers tend to be less effective as parents outside the marriage environment.
- Fathers and mothers are both less effective as parents if there is marital discord.
- When parents agree on decisions and boundaries it helps to legitimise parental authority.
- Cooperative parenting provides modelling which children are likely to imbibe and use in their own relationships with peers. It is important that good communication, mutual respect and mature conflict resolution are modelled well.
- Observing conflict between parents tends to induce stress in children.
- Children can be particularly damaged if they feel they are 'caught in the middle' of a conflict between parents. This can occur if i) one parent speaks negatively about the other in front of the children, ii) children are recruited by one parent as allies against the other or iii) children are asked to convey hurtful messages from one parent to another.
- Conflicts between parents are especially potent if they touch on raw nerves from childhood.

9

Examining the evidence for the impact of spirituality on restoration

Many people report that they derive strength and encouragement from a higher power as they journey along the path to restoration. Is this strength and encouragement real or imagined? If it is real, how can it accessed? These are important questions to answer. We all desire success and happiness and it is important to know if spirituality can help us. Accordingly, this chapter explores these and various other questions.

9.1 The association between spirituality, happiness and mental health

Do spirituality and religious practice affect our happiness and well-being? Many studies seem to suggest that they do. A review of these studies is provided in (Comah, 2013). Spirituality and religious practice correlate positively with a variety of well-being measures such as life satisfaction and happiness (Levin et al, 1996). Studies also show that there is a positive correlation between church attendance and reduced levels of depression among adults, young people and children. Additionally, those who are actively engaged with spirituality and religion are more likely to recover from mental health problems (Comah, 2013).

Are all forms of spiritually assisted restoration equally effective?

It is fairly clear from the research that the answer to this question is "No". Some forms are helpful and some are actually harmful. The most effective form of spirituality is one in which the subject believes that God is working collaboratively with them to help them overcome their problems (Comah, 2013). That is, restoration and happiness are most likely to occur among people who believe they are in a personal relationship with a caring and supportive God.

The above finding is consistent with the investigations within the Grant Study of Adult Development. The Grant Study found that the most striking example of recovery was Godfrey Minot Camille. He described the key turning point in his recovery to be a 14 month stay in hospital which convinced him that "Somebody with a capital 'S' cared about him". He identified that somebody as God. Camille eventually returned to the church of his youth to nurture what he believed was a personal relationship with God (Vaillant. 2013).

> CASE STUDY: Isaac Newton had what many would consider to be a disastrous start in life. His father died while Isaac was still in the womb, and at the age of three Isaac's mother sent him away to live elsewhere. She had re-married and her new husband did not want to care for Isaac. The boy was therefore left with his grandmother.
>
> Despite his challenging start in life, Isaac went on to produce arguably the greatest scientific advances in history. How was it that Newton was able to recover from such an inauspicious start to life?
>
> Newton's diaries and writings may provide some of the answers. He appears to have had a strong personal relationship with God. On one occasion in his diary, for example, he identified those things that were coming between himself and God:

> "Setting my heart on money, learning, pleasure more than thee".
>
> So enamoured was he by God that he wrote much more about theology and the things of God than he did about the physical and mathematical sciences for which he is best known.
>
> He also understood the importance of a responsible relationship with God and of facing his wrong actions and wrong attitudes. His diary entry at the age of 19, for example, records remorse for his threat to burn down the house of his mother and step-father.
>
> Isaac also soaked up fatherly care from a number of practical substitute sources. One of these was the principal of the school he attended. This man took an interest in Isaac and made a place for him at his home.
>
> Isaac additionally benefited from the nurturing environment at Cambridge University. While there, Isaac received substantial amounts of fatherly mentoring and it was one of his mentors who eventually recommended that Newton be given the Lucasian Chair of Mathematics.
>
> Isaac was not perfect and, as with most people, some aspects of his life were dysfunctional. Nonetheless, he still managed to rise above his tragic early circumstances and substantially change history.

9.2 The impact of spirituality on prevention and treatment of substance abuse

In 2001 a major study was conducted by the National US Centre for Addiction and Substance Abuse (CASA), located at Columbia University. CASA performed analyses of data from the National Household Survey, the General Social Survey and a specially conducted Teen Survey. They also extensively reviewed more than 300 publications examining the link between spirituality, religion and recovery from addiction. The significance of the findings from that study was captured in the words of the CASA President (CASA, 2001):

> If ever the sum were greater than the parts, it is in combining the power of God, religion and spirituality with the power of science and professional medicine to prevent and treat substance abuse and addiction.
>
> Joseph A. Califano, Jr., CASA President. (2001).

The CASA study found that people who obtained help from professionals as well as from spiritual support groups, such as AA, were significantly more likely to recover from addictions. It also found that people who successfully recovered from addictions tended to have greater spirituality and faith than those who did not recover (CASA, 2001).

The power of religion and spirituality appears even stronger for prevention than it is for recovery. When CASA compared those who valued religious beliefs with those who did not, it found that adults who attached little weight to religious beliefs were approximately:

i) three times as likely to binge drink,
ii) one and a half times as likely to smoke,
iii) four times as likely to use an illegal drug other than marijuana and
iv) six times more likely to use marijuana.

CASA also compared adults who attended a religious service at least once a week with those who never attended. They found that those who never attended were approximately:

i) seven times as likely to binge drink,
ii) three times as likely to smoke,
iii) five times as likely to use an illegal drug other than marijuana and
iv) eight times as likely to use marijuana.

CASE STUDY: David Wilkerson was a man who realised that he had a responsibility to not only father his own family but also to provide fatherly care for the wider community around him. At one point in his life he became convinced that he needed to go to New York City to help those who were struggling with drug addiction.

One of those he encountered in New York was a man named Nicky Cruz. Nicky was born in 1938 to a Puerto Rican family that practised witchcraft. Nicky's father abused him physically and emotionally and used to lock him in a room with pigeons. When he was locked in the room Nicky would agitate the pigeons by screaming and then they would swarm down and scratch him. His mother also badly mistreated Nicky, regularly beating and taunting him. During one of her trances she even declared him to be the "Son of Satan".

At the age of 15 Nicky was sent to New York City to live with his brother. Shortly after arriving, however, Nicky dropped out of school and his brother subsequently drove him out of the house.

To survive on the streets, Nicky turned to crime. He soon joined the Mau Mau's, one of New York's most violent and notorious gangs. Nicky recounts that, because of the beatings he received as a child, he relished hurting others. This drive to inflict pain on others fuelled his rapid rise to the position of gang leader, where he presided over an orgy of violence, sex and drug abuse.

Almost everyone was afraid of Nicky and very few dared to challenge him. David Wilkerson, however, was not afraid. He told Nicky that God loved him and would never stop loving him. Nicky had no concept of love and was mightily affronted. He struck Wilkerson and threatened to kill him. Wilkerson responded by saying that Nicky could cut him into a thousand pieces but that every piece would continue to declare "I love you".

Wilkerson's words haunted Nicky and for two weeks he could not sleep, thinking all the while about love. At the end of those two weeks Cruz was still confused and decided to attend one of Wilkerson's church services so that he could rob the collection. When Nicky arrived, however, Wilkerson started to talk about a man named Jesus and the suffering he endured when he died on the cross. Nicky had never heard the story, but he felt a deep connection with this man who had been hurt so much, just like him. His heart melted at that point and he started to experience a profound love.

The next day Nicky and some of his gang took their weapons to the police. In time, Wilkerson prayed for the gang, and they experienced a further sense of deep love. Remarkably, this sense of love triggered a sudden and effortless release from their heroin addictions.

From that point on Nicky pursued a new kind of life. He embraced a personal relationship with God. He returned to study and this time pursued his studies with a new sense of purpose. He wanted to learn how to help others, who, like him, had been trapped in a world without hope.

> Nicky's transformation also saw him go on to reach out to troubled youth who had drug addictions and other life controlling problems. Because of his own traumatic childhood he was able to emotionally connect with these young people, and as a result he made a difference to many people's lives. Together with Wilkerson, he was part of the birthing of a successful drug recovery program called *Teen Challenge*.

9.3 The mechanisms of restoration

What are the mechanisms by which spirituality operates? Is it simply a belief mechanism or is it more complex? In 1983 a publication was released which goes some way to answering this question.

The publication in question was an extensive study on alcoholism – one of the most influential such investigations ever conducted (Vaillant, 1983). That study reported that those alcoholics who are successful in their quest for restoration tend to exhibit four key characteristic behaviours on the path to wholeness. Those four behaviours are described below.

i) They find a source of inspiration and hope such as a religious group.
ii) They form new and close relationships (in a support group or elsewhere).
iii) They experience and acknowledge the painful consequences of their alcoholism (often triggered by such confronting circumstances as legal problems or health difficulties).
iv) They find a substitute focus to replace their focus on alcohol.

It was pointed out in (Vaillant, 1983) that all four of these behaviours are nurtured and encouraged in Alcoholics Anonymous. These four behavioural characteristics also suggest four key mechanisms by which spirituality can help those in need of restoration. These key mechanisms are:

i) the inspirational belief mechanism,
ii) the supportive community mechanism,
iii) the conviction mechanism and
iv) the focus (or worship) mechanism.

The inspirational belief mechanism

Most of us understand that beliefs affect outcomes, but just how do beliefs translate into outcomes?

> CASE STUDY: It has been known for a long time that dolphins are able to mimic tricks they are shown. Are they capable of more than just mimicry, though? Could they devise new tricks on their own? In the late 1960s some people started to believe they might well be able to.
>
> Their beliefs prompted some trainers and researchers at Sea Life Park in Hawaii to try an experiment. They started giving a dolphin a reward every time it showed some innovative behaviour. After a while the dolphin started to catch on. It realised that it was being rewarded for innovation and changed its thinking and behaviour. These mental and behavioural changes in the dolphin started slowly but gathered pace over time. Eventually the dolphin reached the point where it was able to perform its own new trick every day.

In the above case study, the dolphin started to develop high levels of creativity when its trainers started believing in it. The trainers' belief prompted the dolphin to change its thinking and behaviour. That is how belief operates. It affects thinking and behaviour in ourselves and/or others.

Beliefs also drive the imagination. This is important because the social science research shows that when someone imagines themselves accomplishing a task, they tend to find it easier to actually accomplish it (Gregory et al, 1982). A belief in success tends to propel a person to success. A belief that a higher power is assisting us can inspire us to believe in higher order outcomes, thereby making higher order outcomes more likely.

Many people struggle to make adjustments to their spiritual beliefs and thinking by themselves. They need 'trainers' to help them, just as the dolphin did. Fathers, both biological and substitute ones, tend to make excellent trainers (Fertfam, 2000; Bruce and Bruce, 1996). A US study found that if both parents attended Sunday School with their children then 72% of the children went on to attend church as adults. If only the father attended Sunday School then 55% of the children attended as adults. By contrast, if only the mother attended Sunday School then 15% of the children attended as adults. If neither parent attended Sunday School then only 6% attended church as adults (Bruce and Bruce, 1996).

Another US study found that if a child is the first person in the family to become a believer, then there is a 3.5% chance that the rest of the family will follow. If the mother is the first person in the family to become a believer, then there is a 17% chance that the rest of the family will follow. If the father is the first person in the family to become a believer, then there is a 93% chance that the rest of the family will follow (Horner et al, 1996).

There is a dilemma associated with the inspirational belief mechanism. Belief in a higher power is helpful for improving the life outcomes of those with poor father-child relationships. At the same time, people who are not close to their father or who had poor 'training' from him are less likely to be inspired to believe in a higher power. For this reason, those with poor father-child relationships need to find spiritual mentors who can act as substitute fathers, particularly in the early stages of their journey.

This book does *not* attempt to explore the evidence for

i) whether a higher power actually does exist and
ii) whether such existence (quite apart from the belief dimension) can assist the restoration process.

It would be difficult to do justice to the above questions in a short space and it is not the objective of this book.

The supportive community mechanism

Religious practice often has a strong communal element to it. Believers typically seek to congregate regularly to encourage and support one another. This gathering process, if done well, can provide a well-spring of caring social fabric to funnel life into broken lives. Studies suggest that this type of community dynamic can assist substantially in recovery from addictions (Atkins and Hawdon, 2007; Vaillant, 1983).

Of course, communities are challenging to maintain. Conflicts frequently arise within voluntary associations of people. Special precautions need to be taken to ensure that communities can survive this conflict and a key way to do this is to establish a culture of forgiveness and charity (Linden and Maercker, 2011; Worthington, E, 2004). Religious and other communities which place an emphasis on forgiveness and charity have a great natural asset in supporting restoration.

CASE STUDY: This case study recounts the story of Roman Pazniewski one evening after he dropped off his daughter at her youth group. Roman has provided the story in his own words.

I saw the assistant priest Fr J. talking with a dishevelled man in worn clothing and long unkempt hair, so I went and said hello to them both. Fr J. introduced me to John, the homeless man, telling me that John was passing through and was having difficulty finding accommodation for the night. He said that they were waiting to hear from Vinnies if there was anything available. After a few minutes, I excused myself and started driving home.

Driving home, I reflected that it would be highly unlikely for Vinnies to find accommodation for anyone on a Friday evening and I suddenly felt a Godly conviction that I should invite John to stay the night at my place. "How can I do that?" I asked God. "I don't know him at all, I have a wife and two daughters at home, what if he turns out to be the axe murderer … or worse?"

However the conviction remained on my heart, so I called Halina and asked if it would be ok to invite a guest over for the night? She readily agreed without asking for details (unusual).

I promptly did a u turn and returned to where John and Fr J were still waiting and invited John to stay the night at my place. John readily accepted the offer, and threw his backpack into my car.

I have to tell you that I was having misgivings already.

John's body odour was powerful, and I had to wind down all the windows to prevent myself gagging. At home Halina had prepared the spare bed, and a meal, and we spent the evening talking with John and listening to his story, which was incredibly sad. It was very late by the time John had said all he wanted to share and went to bed.

The next morning, John joined us for breakfast, and I could not recognise him. He had shaved, trimmed his hair and combed it, his clothes seemed presentable, and he looked bright, fresh and cheerful. He told us that the previous day had been the lowest point in his life, and that he had been considering suicide. Spending the evening in a family home with an attentive audience and a warm meal and a comfortable bed had made the difference to him, and he was going to face the future with a renewed positive outlook.

It was worth taking a risk, and putting up with some inconvenience to meet a treasure like John.

Roman Pazniewski

CASE STUDY: In her book, *Healing Prayer*, Barbara Schlemon recounted the story of a woman living in the US who discovered one day that her son had run away from home. She was emotionally devastated and really struggled to cope. She found it especially difficult to deal with the fact that she had no idea where her son was.

The pain and anguish eventually drove the woman to pray.

> As she prayed she had a sense that God wanted her to do two things. The first was to stop fuelling her anger by making regular negative comments about her son and the second was to write a love letter to the son.
>
> She could not send the letter, but the act of writing it was an opportunity to start practising a new and more forgiving way of relating to her son.
>
> A short time after she had started doing these two things the woman received a phone call. The call was from her son. As he spoke to her he told her that his life had become pretty messed up, but that he had recently met some Christians who were helping him get his life back together. He told her that he was not ready to come home yet, but that he had rung to let her know that he was ok.
>
> A sense of overwhelming relief came upon the woman. Curiously, her forgiveness and change of attitude coincided with a re-parenting of her son by a community of others.

The conviction mechanism

To overcome a problem such as alcoholism or emotional dysfunction we first have to be convicted that we really do have a problem. This conviction often comes to us in part by experiencing the painful consequences of our actions. This could be, perhaps, a confrontation with the law or a major sickness. A good social environment can also strengthen that sense of conviction.

An advantage of programs such as AA is that members are strongly encouraged to face their problems. At the beginning of an AA meeting one of the members will often declare to the group that they are an alcoholic. Some social environments, sadly, have a diametrically opposite ethos to AA. They celebrate escapism. There are a good many contemporary peer groups where people win social kudos by boasting about 'getting wasted' or 'getting lucky'.

Authentically functioning religious groups provide an ethical framework that encourages people to face problems (at least in principle). There are a huge number of scriptural exhortations to not only acknowledge wrong actions, but also to confess them humbly to others. The Book of James, for example, exhorts people to, "Confess your sins one to another". Being immersed in this kind of environment is sometimes enough to push people over the barriers of denial and complacency. Then they can start to deal with their problems.

> CASE STUDY: Mark Ellis understood that the conviction mechanism was important for preventing problems, not just fixing them. Because of this, he looked for ways to foster convictions in his children from a young age.
>
> He and his wife, Sally, found that timing was important. It was not the right time to instruct his children on right and wrong when they were arguing or having power struggles. A much better time was just before bed, when there could be tender interactions between parent and child.
>
> One year, when his son, Sam, was 14 and his son, Nate, was 11, Mark led a family devotional on the Book of Proverbs. It was not always easy talking to his sons about right and wrong; and sometimes during the family devotionals Mark wondered if his efforts were having any effect at all.
>
> Ten years after he had led the devotional on the Book of Proverbs Mark rang his son, Sam, to do an experiment. He asked his son if he remembered anything from the discussion on Proverbs. Sam said that he remembered talking about the sluggard and how it was important to work hard. He also remembered talking about finding a good wife.

> Two things were remembered from 10 years earlier ... Mark took heart that he hadn't been wasting his time.

The focus (or worship) mechanism

Worship is, in essence, intense and prolonged focus. It is the giving of oneself as fully and completely as possible to the object of the worship. Repeated acts of intense focus (worship) cause a person's brain maps to change. The neural pathways become adapted to the object of the focus (Doidge, 2007; Pascual-Leone and Torres, 1993). If a person elects to pursue an intense focus on the God of perfect love the mind becomes increasingly consumed with love. The ability to give and receive love increases. This phenomenon is essentially the focus (or worship) mechanism.

The power of worship is supported by a study performed among three generations of Mexican Americans. The finding was that regular religious worship practice in the two oldest generations correlated with increased life satisfaction in the oldest two generations. The study also showed that regular worship in the older generations had a positive longitudinal effect on reducing depression in the youngest generation (Levin et al, 1996).

Worship of the God of love is important because it is a key tool for expanding love in our lives, the latter being the key driver for happiness and success.

In the absence of a focus on love, a person's mind may well start to focus in a prolonged way on something else, something inferior to love. If this occurs, the mental structures can be strongly affected in a lasting and detrimental way (Doidge, 2007). One common outworking of this detrimental eventuality is the phenomenon of addictions.

When a person is not pre-occupied with love they become more vulnerable to addictions. The latter are stimulated by an intense and prolonged focus on something more base than love. The object of the focus could be self-gratification derived from drugs, alcohol, sex, or pornography. It could be an inordinate preoccupation with power or money or self. It could be other things. Regardless of the object of the focus, the person's mental structures are likely to be adversely affected in the long-term.

> CASE STUDY: French author, Guy de Maupassant, was one of history's foremost writers of short stories. He was very close to his mother, but had a poor relationship with his father. His first novel, *Boule de Souif*, was considered a masterpiece and made him famous. His second novel, *Bel Ami*, had 37 printings in just four months and helped to finance the purchase of his private yacht, also called *Bel Ami*.
>
> De Maupassant was not adept at love in his adult years, nor did he have much interest in religion – his focus lay elsewhere. He was exceedingly promiscuous as a young adult and as a result he contracted syphilis. He travelled widely on his yacht and produced acclaimed and successful novels which brought him great wealth.
>
> De Maupassant's focus on fame, fortune, sex, and even the seemingly noble pursuit of writing failed to bring him much happiness. He attempted suicide, was committed to an asylum and died at the age of 42. He self-penned epitaph captured something of the tragedy of his life:
> "I have coveted everything and taken pleasure in nothing."

The CASA study mentioned earlier in this chapter lends support to the notion that worshipping the God of perfect love is one mechanism which can help reduce vulnerability to addictions. People who regularly attended church were found to be seven times less likely to binge drink, three times less likely to smoke and five times less likely to use an illegal drug other than marijuana (CASA, 2001).

Negative focus

Previous chapters have considered various potential root causes of on-going life problems. One heretofore unconsidered source of problems is involvement in the occult. The destructive potential of occult involvement is supported by an investigation by Tennant-Clark et al. in the journal, *Adolescent* (Tennant-Clark et al, 1989). That study found that there was a significant correlation between occult involvement in adolescents and

i) drug use,
ii) poor self-image and
iii) low self-confidence.

As alluded to earlier, prolonged and intense focus affects the brain's neural pathways. If the object of that focus happens to be negative to the point of being devilish (as occurs in the case of occult involvement), then the person moves towards something explicitly evil. This kind of engagement opens the way for sorrow and grief to enter a person's life.

9.4 Empathic capacity

The Grant Study found that empathic capacity correlated with every major aspect of human flourishing – economic success, physical health, mental health, happiness and successful relationships (Vaillant, 2012; Vaillant, 2013). The practice of empathising with others, then, appears to be very important. We all like to feel that others care about how we think and feel. That is why empathy matters.

Empathic engagement has different implications for different people. Some people are already over-empathising and wearing themselves out emotionally. Those people need to pace themselves better and learn to hone the use of their emotional resources. Other people under-engage empathically. This can cause problems in their relationships. Family and friends are likely to sense their lack of care. These under-engagers need to start practising empathy more wholeheartedly. They need to enter more fully into the world of others.

The inescapable reality, of course, is that if we emotionally connect with others we will at times get hurt. Empathy therefore has to go hand in hand with mature coping mechanisms such as forgiveness and open communication.

John and Paula Sandford are writers who have long advocated active practice of empathy in relationships. They, however, have gone further and argued for a synergistic melding of empathic engagement with another evidence based practice, namely, active belief in a collaborative and caring God (Sandford, 2007). They argue that those who believe in a loving God have a responsibility to empathise with others (i.e. actively sense the needs of others) and bring those needs to God in prayer. They call this synergistic melding 'burden bearing'.

While the Sandfords argue for the importance and effectiveness of burden bearing, they also issue a caveat. Burden bearing needs to be pursued judiciously, otherwise the burden bearer can be crushed by the excessive weight of the burden(s).

In their writings the Sandfords point out that not everyone is born with the same capacity for burden bearing. Some people have a particularly strong natural gift in this area. They refer to these people as 'natural burden bearers'. They claim that these natural burden bearers typically have

i) above average sensitivity,
ii) above average creativity,
iii) heightened perception and
iv) an above average awareness of the consequences of wrong-doing.

The Sandfords claim that it is quite common for natural burden bearers to take on too many burdens and to suffer excessively as a result. This can sometimes lead to:

i) a tendency to take an unusually long time to find their own identity, and

ii) a tendency to resort to destructive coping mechanisms, including addictions such as alcohol abuse.

> CASE STUDY: British Psychiatrist, Kenneth McCall, recounts a story in his book, *Healing the family tree*, about a young girl whom he treated. The girl was exhibiting highly dysfunctional behaviour and her parents asked McCall to see if he could help her.
>
> As the doctor talked with the young girl she began making some startling comments. Among other things, she claimed that she was upset about her parents flushing her sister, Melissa, down the toilet. When McCall relayed this comment to the parents they were amazed. The mother had actually had a miscarriage and the parents had decided to call the child lost in the miscarriage, Melissa. The parents, however, had never mentioned the miscarriage or the name of the lost child to their young daughter.
>
> McCall suggested to the parents that they had probably never grieved properly for the loss of their unborn child. Their young daughter was one of those children who was especially sensitive and perceptive. She had actually picked up on the tragedy of the miscarriage, even though she had never been told about it.
>
> The young girl was too inexperienced to know how to deal with the burden she was carrying and so McCall advised the

> parents to organise a grieving service and to pray to God to lift the burden of the tragic miscarriage. This the parents did and the young girl's behaviour problems immediately disappeared.

The Sandfords suggest that in order to avoid the pitfall of taking on excessive burdens, natural burden bearers need to maintain some balance. They should not abandon the process of burden bearing completely, but they should bear only selected burdens from others and then carry (outsource) these to God in prayer. Ultimately, the whole process should be an enriching, rather than overwhelming process. If natural burden bearers cultivate and practise their gift wisely, they can convey unusually powerful warmth and love.

9.5 Turning 'lemons into lemonade'

The Grant Study found that the happiest people tended to accept the 'lemons' life handed them and went about turning them into 'lemonade' (Vaillant, 2002). Other studies have found that people who believe in a caring and collaborative God also tend to have above average happiness (Comah, 2013). During the 1970s and 1980s, Merlin Carothers wrote a series of books which promoted the notion of synergistically combining a 'lemons into lemonade' predisposition with belief in a caring and collaborative God (Carothers, 1970; Carothers, 1980; Carothers, 1984).

Carothers encouraged his readers to see their difficulties as opportunities rather than problems and to seek God's help to make the best of these opportunities. He urged people to give thanks in *all* circumstances and to systematically praise God for *everything* in their lives, good and bad.

The message found a resonance with many people and his books sold millions of copies. As people began to follow Carothers' advice, many remarkable stories began to filter back.

> CASE STUDY: Jim was a man who had an alcoholic father. Jim's dad was unwilling to acknowledge that he had a problem with alcohol abuse and would get angry if anyone brought up the subject.
>
> Jim prayed for thirty years for his father to overcome his problems to no avail. One day Jim heard a message about the benefits of praising God in *all* circumstances, and eventually it occurred to him that he had never thanked and praised God for his father's alcoholism. He talked with his wife about this, and together they decided to do some experimenting. They spent the day thanking and praising God for their father's debilitating problem with alcohol.
>
> The next day Jim and his wife had their parents over for their usual weekly dinner, and the father uncharacteristically lingered after the dinner and started talking. He said that he had read an article about the Jesus revolution and wondered whether there was anything in it. A lengthy discussion followed about Christianity.
>
> Within a couple of weeks the father acknowledged his problem with alcohol. He turned to God for help and successfully recovered from his addiction. Jim and his wife marvelled at the fact that they had prayed for thirty years for God to heal their father of his alcoholism and nothing happened. They thanked and praised God for just one day for the alcoholism and the problem was solved.

It is intriguing to wonder why expressing gratitude and praise for something as seemingly horrible as alcoholism could have such an effect. Perhaps it is because we need to see value in the 'lemons' before we turn them into 'lemonade'.

If we can accept that the supreme being of this universe is perfectly wise, then it follows that he knows just how crucial it is to accept the cards life deals us and to do the best we can with those cards. It is not unreasonable, then, that he might set up a reward system which would encourage that kind of attitude.

9.6 Summary

- Studies reveal a significant correlation between spirituality/religious practice and happiness, well-being and mental health.
- Not all forms of spirituality are equally effective. The most effective form is one in which people believe they are in a collaborative relationship with a caring God.
- It is postulated that there are four key spiritual mechanisms which assist the restoration process: the conviction mechanism, the supportive community mechanism, the inspirational belief mechanism and the focus (or worship) mechanism.
- The inspirational belief mechanism is strongly influenced by the modelling provided by parents, particularly the father.
- People are less likely to begin taking harmful drugs if they place value on religious beliefs.
- People who believe in a higher power are significantly more likely to recover from physical addictions, provided that professional help is sought as well.
- Restoration of happiness, well-being and mental health tends to be quicker for those who believe in a higher power.
- Maturity requires a disposition towards turning 'lemons into lemonade' and for those who believe in God there is benefit in thanking and praising God for the 'lemons'.

- There is long-term benefit in being sensitive to the needs of others and for those who believe in a higher power, this should translate to a commitment to pray for the needs of others.

10

Conclusions

This book has looked at the evidence for what it is that fosters success and happiness in life. It has been found that a person's relationships with their parents are extremely important. Because father-child relationships have tended to break down in contemporary society more than mother-child ones this book has concentrated on the former.

The role of fathers has been examined in the light of the evidence. It has been found that the involvement of the father affects almost every key domain of well-being – the mental, emotional, physical, professional, moral and spiritual. The early years between conception and six years of age are particularly important, while adolescence is quite important as well. The effect of the father's involvement is usually positive, although a combative and uncaring father can actually be a negative influence.

If a child has a poor relationship with the father throughout childhood there is a strong possibility that the child will grow up to have significant life problems. The good news is that, according to the evidence, the child can overcome those life problems with proactive action. This pro-active action is constituted of two parts: forgiveness is the first part and the second is a commitment to pursue a Twelve Step type restoration process. The restoration process is expedited by adopting a willingness to turn 'lemons into lemonade' and by accepting the challenge of emotionally engaging with others, even if that means getting hurt in the process.

If a child does have major life problems, wise and caring parental intervention can help considerably. Natural parents are not the only ones who can intervene. Substitute parents can also do much good.

The power of spirituality in recovery from both physical addictions and impoverished childhoods has been examined. It has been found that when combined with professional help, spirituality is linked to significantly higher recovery rates. Not all forms of spirituality, however, are equally effective. Studies suggest that the most successful form of spirituality is one in which people believe they are in a collaborative personal relationship with a caring God.

Spirituality is postulated to operate via four key mechanisms

i) the inspirational belief mechanism

ii) the supportive community mechanism,

iii) the conviction mechanism and

iv) the focus (or worship) mechanism.

10.1 Where to from here?

The end goal is love, for it is only love which leads to happiness, success and fulfilment in life. There are a number of gate-keeper factors, however, which moderate our ability to give and receive love. Chief among these are the father factor, the mother factor and the addiction factor.

Thomas Edison committed to becoming a successful inventor so that he could improve his mother's quality of life. He ended up improving the quality of life of people all around the world. Alexander Graham Bell went to significant effort to improve his mother's ability to communicate. He ended up ushering in a communications revolution. Theodore Roosevelt entered a life of service to help honour the memory of his late father. He himself ended up being honoured for his service to the world at large, even winning a Nobel Prize.

Our happiness is bound up with our calling to make the world a better place. To achieve our potential, though, we must master the gate-keeper factors. This means resolving our relationships with our parents and gradually bringing our addictions to power, money, sex and self-gratification under control. Some have tried to short-cut this process. Adolf Hitler and Josef Stalin are extreme examples. They tried to change the world without first resolving their relationships with their parents or dealing with their compulsive addictions to power and control. The results were tragic.

This book has provided some reflections and provocations for those wishing to master the gate-keeper functions which lead to love. We, the authors, are well aware that many others are currently providing a much better example of love than us. We also know that others may well have better ideas and more inspiring stories than we have. To tap into the rich social fabric of wisdom and love existing among our readers, we have set up an interactive web-site. We would like to invite interested readers to place their thoughts, reflections, stories, photos and exhortations on that site: www.menalive.org.au/fatherfactor

It is important to remember that we cannot navigate the journey to wholeness by ourselves. We need to proactively connect with others who can love us, support us and challenge us. We encourage our readers to make the necessary connections, be they within an extended family, a vibrant church, a support group, a counselling organisation or elsewhere.

We have also provided a list of resources and some contact points for counselling and support groups in Appendix III. We hope that the resources available in the appendix and on the web-site might be a source of healing, encouragement and solace for all of us on the journey.

We conclude finally by re-visiting the story of Godfrey Minot Camille, the most startling example of restoration in the Grant Study of Adult Development.

CASE STUDY: Godfrey Minot Camille grew up in a family that was cold, distant and un-nurturing. As a result he developed many life problems. He was a hypochondriac, he hated his job, he suffered ongoing problems with depression, he attempted suicide and he had a number of tragically failed relationships.

Camille was eventually able to overcome his problems by attacking them on many fronts. He started by seeking counselling. This helped him to deal with his many neuroses. He then developed an interest in genealogy, and through this interest, contacted much of his extended family. In so doing he built up around himself the nurturing family he lacked as a child. He availed himself of the power of spiritually assisted restoration and returned to the church of his youth where he nurtured a personal relationship with a caring God. He became actively involved in his church community and gave and received love through it. He used his job as a physician to help others and to receive nurture from them. He also invested heavily in his own children and his wife.

Camille began to see progress as soon as he started facing and dealing with his problems. His transformation, though, was gradual. Like Camille, we are likely to experience progress as soon as we start to confront and proactively deal with our problems. Our journey to wholeness will also be gradual, but it is likely to be filled with many rewarding moments.

References

Alcdiv. (2012). "Alcohol and divorce statistics", USA. (http://www.edivorcestatistics.com/alcohol.html Accessed 16th January, 2014).

Alfaro, E., Umana-Taylor, A. and Bamaca, M. (2006). "The influence of academic support on Latino adolescents' academic motivation", *Family Relations*, 55: 279-291.

Allen, S. and Daly, K. (2007). "The Effects of father involvement: An updated research summary of the evidence". (http://fira.ca/cms/documents/29/Effects_of_Father_Involvement.pdf Accessed, 14th February, 2014).

Allen, S. and Hawkins, A. (1999). "Mothers' beliefs and behaviours that inhibit greater father involvement in family", *Journal of Marriage and the Family*, 61: 199-212.

Amato, P. (1987). *Children in Australian families: The growth of competence*, New York: Prentice-Hall.

Amato, P. (1989). "Family processes and the competence of primary school children and adolescents", *Journal of Youth and Adolescence*, 18: 39-53.

Amato, P. (1993). "Children's adjustment to divorce: Theories, hypotheses, and empirical support", *Journal of Marriage and the Family*, 55: 23-38.

Amato, P. (1994). "Father-child relationships, mother-child relations, and offspring psychological well-being in early adulthood", *Journal of Marriage and the Family*, 56: 1031-1042.

Amato, P. (1998). "More than money? Men's contributions to their children's lives", in A. Booth and A. Crouter (Eds.), *Men in families: When do they get involved? What difference does it make?* (pp. 241-278), Mahwah, NJ: Lawrence Erlbaum Associates, Publisher.

Amato, P. (2005). "The Impact of Family Formation Change on the Cognitive, Social, and Emotional Well-Being of the Next Generation". (http://files.eric.ed.gov/fulltext/EJ795852.pdf Accessed, 27th July, 2014).

Amato, P. and Booth, A. (1997). *A generation at risk: Growing up in an era of family upheaval*, Cambridge, MA: Harvard University Press.

Amato, P. and Gilbreth, J. (1999). "Non-resident fathers and children's well-being: A meta-analysis", *Journal of Marriage and the Family*, 61: 557-573.

Amato, P. and Rivera, F. (1999). "Paternal involvement and children's behavior problems", *Journal of Marriage and the Family*, 61: 375-384.

Andrews, K. (2012). *Maybe I Do,* Connor Court.

Argys, L., Peters, H., Brooks-Gunn, J. and Smith, J. (1998). "The impact of child support on cognitive outcomes of young children", *Demography*, 35: 159-172.

Astone, N. and McLanahan, S. (1991). "Family structure, parental practices, and high school completion", *American Sociological Review*, 56: 309-320.

Atkins, R. and Hawdon, J. (2007). "Religiosity and participation in mutual-aid support groups for addiction", *Journal of Substance Abuse and Treatment*, 33: 321-331.

Austheal. (2012). "Australia's Health 2012", The Thirteenth Biennial Health Report of the Australian Health and Welfare. (http://books.google.com.au/books?id=1CazE2WqNBEC Accessed 16th January, 2014).

Bachrach, C. and Sonnerstein, F. (1998). "Male fertility and family formation: Research and data on the pathways to fatherhood, in Federal Interagency Forum on Child and Family Statistics, (Eds.), *Nurturing fatherhood: Improving Data and Research on Male Fertility, Family Formation and Fatherhood*, June. (http://fatherhood.hhs.gov/cfsforum/front.htm Accessed 22nd April, 2014).

Bandura, A. (1971). *Social learning theory*, Morristown, NJ: General Learning Press.

Beller, G. and Hernandez, P. (1994). "The effects of child support on educational attainment", in *Child support and child well-being*, edited by I. Garfinkel, S. McLanahan, and P. Robins, Washington, D.C.: Urban Institute Press.

Belsky, J., Steinberg, L. and Draper. P. (1991). "Childhood experience, interpersonal development, and reproductive strategy: An evolutionary theory of socialization", *Child Development*, 62: 647-670.

Berlinsky, E. and Biller, H. (1982). *Parental death and psychological development*, Wiley.

Biller, H. (1993). *Fathers and families: Paternal factors in child development*, Westport, CT: Auborn House.

Biro, B., Greenspan, L., Galvez, M., Pinney, S., Teitelbaum, S., Windham, G., Deardorff, J., Herrick, R., Succop, P., Hiatt, R., Kushi, L. and Wolff, M. (2013). "Onset of breast development in a longitudinal cohort", *Pediatrics*, 132: 1019-1027.

Blaicher, W., Bieglmayer, C., Blicher, A., Knogler, W. and Huber, J. (1999). "The role of oxytocin in relation to female sexual arousal", *Gynecologic and Obstetric Investigation*, 47: 125-126.

Bond, J., Kaskutas, L. and Weisner, C. (2003). "The persistent influence of social networks and Alcoholics Anonymous on abstinence", *Journal of Studies on Alcohol*, 64: 579-588.

Bouchard, G. and Lee, C. (2000). "The marital context for father involvement with their pre-school children: The role of partner support", *Journal of Prevention and Intervention in the Community*, 2: 37-54.

Brandsma, J., Maultsby, M., Jr. and Welsh, R. (1980). *Outpatient Treatment of Alcoholism: A review and comparative study*, Baltimore, MD: University Park Press.

Bronfenbrenner, U. (1990). "Discovering what families do", in *Rebuilding the Nest*, D. Blankenhorn, S. Bayme and J. Bethke Elshtain, Eds., p. 34.

Bruce, R. and Bruce, D. (1996). *Becoming spiritual soulmates with your child*, Nashville: Broadman and Holman. p. 52.

Carothers, M. (1970). *Prison to praise*, Carothers Publishing.

Carothers, M. (1980). *Power in praise*, Carothers Publishing.

Carothers, M. (1984). *Bringing heaven into hell*, Carothers Publishing.

CASA. (2001). "So help me God: Substance abuse, religion and spirituality", Report from The National Centre on Addiction and Substance Abuse at Columbia University. (http://www.casacolumbia.org/articlefiles/379-So%20Help%20Me%20God.pdf Accessed 22nd April, 2014).

Cdc. (2010). "Adverse childhood experiences reported by adults". (2010). (www.cdc.gov/mmwr/preview/mmwrhtml/mm5949a1.htm Accessed 14th January, 2014).

Cobb-Clark, D. and Tekin, E. (2011). "Fathers and youths' delinquent behaviour". (http://melbourneinstitute.com/downloads/working_paper_series/wp2011n23.pdf Accessed 11th February, 2014).

Comah, D. (2013). "The impact of spirituality on mental health", Mental Health Foundation, United Kingdom. (http://www.mentalhealth.org.uk/content/assets/PDF/publications/impact-spirituality.pdf?view=Standard Accessed 22nd April, 2014).

Connors, G., Tonigan, J. and Miller, W. (2001). "A longitudinal model of intake symptomatology, AA participation, and outcome: retrospective study of the Project MATCH outpatient and aftercare samples", *Journal of Studies on Alcohol*, 62: 817-825.

Cov. (2013). "250+ facts and statistics about pornography". (http://www.covenanteyes.com/pornography-facts-and-statistics/ Accessed 15th January, 2013).

Csikszentmihalyi, M. (1996). *Creativity: Flow and the Psychology of Discovery and Invention*, New York: Harper Perennial.

Dawson, D., Grant, B., Stinson, F. and Chou, P. (2006). "Estimating the effect of help-seeking on achieving recovery from alcohol dependence", *Addiction*, 101: 824-834.

Doidge, N. (2007). *The brain that changes itself*, Penguin.

Driessen, E. and Hollon, S. (2010). "Cognitive behavioral therapy for mood disorders: Efficacy, moderators and mediators", *Psychiatric Clinics of North America*, 33: 537-555.

Dubowitz, H., Black, M., Cox, C., Kerr, M., Litrownik, A., Radhakrishna, A., English, D., Wood Schneider, M. and Runyan, D. (2001). "Father involvement and children's functioning at age six years: A multisite study", *Child Maltreatment*, 6: 300-309.

Easterbrooks, M. and Goldberg, W. (1990). "Security of toddler-parent attachment: Relation to children's sociopersonality functioning during kindergarten", in B. Ellis, J. Bates and L. Woodward. (2003). "Does father absence place girls at greater risk for early sexual activity and teen pregnancy?", *Child Development*, 74: 801-821.

Ellis, B. and Garber, J. (2000). "Psychosocial antecedents of variation in girls' pubertal timing: Maternal depression, stepfather presence, and marital and family stress", *Child Development*, 71: 485-501.

Erickson, J. (2011). "Why mothers matter". (www.mercatornet.com/articles/view/why_mothers_matter Accessed 22nd April, 2014).

Ericsson, K. (2005). "Recent advances in expertise research: A commentary on the contributions to the special issue", *Applied Cognitive Psychology*, 19: 233-241.

Ericsson, K., Krampe, R. and Tesch-Romer, C. (1993). "The role of deliberate practice in the acquisition of expert performance", *Psychological Review*, 100: 363-406.

Ferguson, N. (2005). "Heaven knows how we will re-kindle our religion but I believe we must". *The Telegraph*, July. (http://www.telegraph.co.uk/comment/personal-view/3618721/Heaven-knows-how-well-rekindle-our-religion-but-I-believe-we-must.html Accessed 22nd April 2014).

Ferri, M., Amato, L. and Davoli, M. (2006). "Alcoholics Anonymous and other 12-step programmes for alcohol dependence", *Cochrane Database of Systematic Reviews*, 3, Article No. CD005032.

Fertfam. (2000). "Fertility and Family Survey", conducted by the Federal Statistical Office (Switzerland).

Field, T., Lang, C., Yando, R. and Bendell, R. (1995). "Adolescents' intimacy with parents and friends", *Adolescence*, 30: 133-140.

Finkelhor, D., Hotaling, G., Lewis, A. and Smith, C. (1990). "Sexual abuse in a national survey of men and women: prevalence, characteristics and risk factors", *Child Abuse and Neglect*, 14: 19-28.

Flouri, E. (2005). *Fathering and child outcomes*, West Sussex, England: John Wiley and Sons Ltd.

Flouri, E. and Buchanan, A. (2002). "Childhood predictors of labor force participation in adult life", *Journal of Family and Economic Issues*, 23: 101-120

Formoso, D., Gonzales, N., Barrera, M. and Dumka, L. (2007). "Interparental relations, maternal employment, and fathering in Mexican American families", *Journal of Marriage and Family*, 69: 26-39.

Fortney, J., Booth, B., Zhang, M., Humphrey, J. and Wiseman, E. (1998). "Controlling for selection bias in the evaluation of Alcoholics Anonymous as aftercare treatment", *Journal of Studies on Alcohol*, 59: 690-697.

Franz, C., McClelland, D. and Weinberger, J. (1991). "Childhood antecedents of conventional social accomplishments in midlife adults: A 35-year prospective study", *Journal of Personality and Social Psychology*, 60: 586-595.

Freeman, W. (1995). *Societies of brains: A study in the neuroscience of love and hate*, Lawrence Erlbaum Associates Publishers, USA.

Freeman, W. (1996). "Neuroscientists learn that joy comes through dancing, not drugs", *Journal of Consciousness Studies,* 4: 67-71.

Furstenberg, F. and Cherlin, A. (1991). *Divided families: What happens to children when parents part,* Cambridge, MA: Harvard University Press.

Furstenberg, F. and Harris, K. (1993). "When and why fathers matter: Impacts of father involvement on the children of adolescent mothers", in R. Lerman and T. Ooms (Eds.), *Young unwed fathers: Changing roles and emerging policies* (pp. 117-138), Philadelphia: Temple University Press.

Furstenberg, F., Morgan, S. and Allison, P. (1987). "Paternal participation and children's well-being after marital dissolution", *American Sociological Review,* 52: 695-701.

Fuselier, G. (1999). "Placing the Stockholm Syndrome in perspective", *FBI Law Enforcement Bulletin,* July, pp. 22-25.

Gamer, M., Zurowski, B. and Buchel, C. (2010). "Different amygdala subregions mediate valence-related and attentional effects of oxytocin in humans", *Proceedings of the National Academy of Science,* USA, 107: 9400-9405.

Gatchel, R. and Rollings, K. (2008). "Evidence-informed management of chronic low back pain with cognitive behavioral therapy", *The Spine Journal,* 8: 40-44.

Gillis, C. (2012). "Psychiatrist George Vaillant on secrets to a long life and a bigger salary". (http://www2.macleans.ca/2012/10/04/the-secrets-to-a-long-life-and-a-bigger-salary-and-why-nice-guys-do-finish-first/ Accessed 25th January, 2012).

Gladwell, M. (2008). *Outliers: The story of success,* Little Brown and Company.

Gordon, M. (1990). "The family environment of sexual abuse: A comparison of natural and step-father abuse", *Child Abuse and Neglect,* 13: 121-130.

Gortmaker, S., Must, A., Sobol, A., Peterson, K., Colditz, G. and Dietz, W. (1996). "Television viewing as a cause of increasing obesity among children in the United States, 1986-1990", *Annals of Pediatric Adolescent Medicine,* 150 (4): 356-362.

Gottfredson, M. and Hirschi, T. (1990). *A general theory of crime,* Stanford, CA: Stanford University Press.

Gould, E., Tanapat, P., Rydel, T. and Hastings, N. (2000). "Regulation of hippocampal neurogenesis in adulthood", *Biological Psychiatry,* 48: 715-720.

Greenberg, M., Cicchetti, D. and Cummings, E. (Eds.). *Attachment in the preschool years: Theory, research and intervention* (pp. 221-244), Chicago: University of Chicago Press.

Gregory, W., Cialdini, R. and Carpenter, K. (1982). "Self-relevant scenarios as mediators of likelihood estimates and compliance: does imagining make it so?", *Journal of Personality and Social Psychology*, 43: 88-99.

Guastella, A., Einfeld, S., Gray, K., Rinehart, N., Tonge, B., Lambert, T. and Hickie, I. (2010). "Intranasal oxytocin improves emotion recognition for youth with autism spectrum disorders", *Biological Psychiatry*, 67: 692-694.

Gutiérrez, M., Sánchez, M., Trujillo, A. and Sánchez, L (2009). "Cognitive-behavioral therapy for chronic psychosis", *Actas espanolas de psiquiatria*, 37: 106-114.

Hald, G. (2006). "Gender differences in pornography consumption among young heterosexual Danish adults", *Archives of Sexual Behaviour*, 35: 577-585.

Harper, C. and McLanahan, S. (2004). "Father absence and youth incarceration", *Journal of Research on Adolescence*, 14: 369-397

Hattie, J. (2009). *Visible Learning*, Routledge.

Harris, K., Furstenberg, F. and Marmer, J. (1998). "Paternal involvement with adolescents in intact families: The influence of fathers over the life course", *Demography*, 35: 201-216.

Hassett, A. and Gevirtz, R. (2009). "Non-pharmacologic treatment for fibromyalgia: Patient education, cognitive-behavioral therapy, relaxation techniques, and complementary and alternative medicine", *Rheumatic Disease Clinics of North America*, 35: 393-407.

Horner, B., Ralston, R. and Sunde, D. (1996). *The promise keeper at work*, Promise Builders Study Series, Focus on the Family Publishing, p. 111.

Howard, K., Lefever, J., Borkowski, J. and Whitman, T. (2006). "Fathers' influence in the lives of children with adolescent mothers", *Journal of Family Psychology*, 20: 468-476.

Huffpost. (2013). "Porn Sites Get More Visitors Each Month Than Netflix, Amazon And Twitter Combined", *Huffington Post*, 15-4-2013. See also // blogs.psychcentral.com/sex/2013/05/the-prevalence-of-porn/ (Accessed 13th February, 2014).

Humphreys, K., Mankowski, E., Moos, R. and Finney, J. (1999). "Do enhanced friendship networks and active coping mediate the effect of self-help groups on substance abuse?", *Annals of Behavioral Medicine*, 21: 54-60.

Humphreys, K., Phibbs, C. and Moos, R. (2006). "Addressing self-selection effects in evaluations of mutual help groups and professional mental health services: an introduction to two-stage sample selection models", *Evaluation and Program Planning*, 19: 301-308.

Jaffe, S., Moffitt, T., Caspi, A. and Taylor, A. (2003). "Life with (or without) father: The benefits of living with two biological parents depend on the father's antisocial behaviour", *Child Development*, 74: 109-126.

Jeynes, W. (2001). "The effects of recent parental divorce on their children's sexual attitudes and behaviour", *Journal of Divorce and Remarriage*, 35: 125-133.

Kalyuga, S. (2007). "Expertise reversal effect and its implications for learner-tailored instruction", *Educational Psychology Review*, 19: 509-539.

Kaskutas, L. (2009). "Alcoholics Anonymous effectiveness: faith meets science", *Journal of Addictive Disorders*, 28: 145-157.

Kaskutas, L., Bond J. and Humphreys, K. (2002). "Social networks as mediators of the effect of Alcoholics Anonymous", *Addiction*, 97: 891-900.

Kelly, J., Myers, M. and Brown, S. (2002). "Do adolescents affiliate with 12-step groups? A mulitvariate process model of effects", *Journal of Studies on Alcohol*, 63: 293-304.

Khantzian, E. and Mack, J. (1989). "Alcoholics anonymous and contemporary psychodynamic theory", in M. Galanter Ed., *Recent Developments in Alcoholism*, New York, NY: Plenum Press: pp. 67-89.

Kilgar, M. and Merzenich, M. (1998). "Cortical map reorganisation enabled by nucleus basalis activity", *Science*, 279: 1714-1718.

King, V. (2006). "The antecedents and consequences of adolescents' relationships with stepfathers and non-resident fathers", *Journal of Marriage and Family*, 68: 910-928.

Kotelchuck, M. (1976). "The infant's relationship to the father: experimental evidence", in M. Lamb (Ed.), *The role of the father in child development* (1st Ed., pp. 329-344), New York: Wiley.

Lamb, M. (1997). *The role of the father in child development* (3rd Ed., pp. 1-18). New York: John Wiley and Sons, Inc.

Larson, D., Sherill, K., Lyons, J., Craigie, F., Thielman, S., Greenwold, M. and Larson, S. (1992). "Associations between dimensions of religious commitment and mental health", reported in the *American Journal of Psychiatry* and the *Archives of General Psychiatry*: 1978-1989, *American Journal of Psychiatry*, 149: 557-559.

Larsen, P., Kronenberg, H., Melmed, S. and Polonsky, K., Eds. (2003). "Puberty: Ontogeny, Neuroendocrinology, Physiology, and Disorders", in *Williams' Textbook of Endocrinology*, 10th Ed. (Philadelphia: Saunders), pp. 1115-1286.

Lave, J. and Wenger, E. (1991). *Situated Learning: Legitimate Peripheral Participation*, Cambridge University Press.

Levin, J., Markides, K. and Ray, L. (1996). "Religious attendance and psychological well-being in Mexican Americans: a panel analysis of three-generation's data", *The Gerontologist*, 36: 454-463.

Linden, M. and Maercker, A. (2011). *Embitterment: Societal, Psychological, and Clinical perspectives*, Springer.

Lozoff, M.M. (1974). "Fathers and autonomy in women", in R. Kundsin (Ed.), *Women and success*, (pp. 103-109), New York: Morrow.

McKellar, J., Stewart, E. and Humphreys, K. (2003). "Alcoholics Anonymous involvement and positive alcohol-related outcomes: cause, consequence, or just a correlate? A prospective 2-year study of 2,319 alcohol-dependent men", *Journal of Consulting and Clinical Psychology*, 71: 302-308.

McLanahan, S. and Sandefur, G. (1997). *Growing up with a single parent*, Harvard University Press.

Manning, J. (2004). Senate Testimony, referencing: Dedmon, J., "Is the Internet bad for your marriage? Online affairs, pornographic sites playing greater role in divorces," 2002, Press release from The Dilenschneider Group, Inc.

Marsiglio, W., Amato, P., Day, R. and Lamb, M. (2000). "Scholarship on fatherhood in the 1990s and beyond", *Journal of Marriage and the Family*, 62: 1173–1191.

Matusiewicz, A., Hopwood, C., Banducci, A. and Lejuez, C. (2010). "The effectiveness of Cognitive Behavioral Therapy for personality disorders", *Psychiatric Clinics of North America*, 33: 657-685.

Milne, F. and Judge, D. (2010). "Brothers delay menarche and the onset of sexual activity in their sisters", *Proceedings of the Royal Society*, doi:10.1098/rspb.2010.1377.

Moos, R. and Moos, B. (2006). "Participation in treatment and Alcoholics Anonymous: a 16-year follow-up of initially untreated individuals", *Journal of Clinical Psychology*, 62: 735-750.

Morgenstern, J., Labouvie, E., McCrady, B., Kahler, C. and Frey, R. (1997). "Affiliation with Alcoholics Anonymous following treatment: a study of its therapeutic effects and mechanisms of action", *Journal of Consulting and Clinical Psychology*, 65: 768-777.

Morhenn, V., Beavin, L. and Zak, P. (2012). "Massage increases oxytocin and reduces adrenocorticotropin hormone in humans", *Alternative Therapeutic Health Medicine*, 18: 11-18.

Murphy, M., Seckyl, J., Burton, S. and Lightman, S. (1987). "Changes In Oxytocin and Vasopressin Secretion During Sexual Activity in Men", *Journal of Clinical Endocrinology and Metabolism*, DOI: http://dx.doi.org/10.1210/jcem-65-4-738.

Neuman, E. (2010). "An amazing agent of change", *Haaretz*, April 19th. (http://www.haaretz.com/weekend/week-s-end/an-amazing-agent-of-change-1.284544 Accessed 14th July, 2014).

Otte, C. (2011). "Cognitive behavioral therapy in anxiety disorders: Current state of the evidence", *Dialogues in clinical neuroscience*, 13: 413-421.

Ouimette, P., Moos, R. and Finney, J. (1998). "Influence of outpatient treatment and 12-step group involvement on one-year substance abuse treatment outcomes", *Journal of Studies on Alcohol*, 59: 513-522.

Parker, H. and Parker, S. (1986). "Father-daughter sexual abuse", *American Journal of Orthopsychiatry*, 56: 531-549.

Pascual-Leone, A. and Torres, F. (1993). "Plasticity of of the sensorimotor cortex representation of the reading finger in Braille readers", *Brain*, 116: 39-52.

Parke, M. (2003). *Are Married Parents Really Better for Children? What Research Says About the Effects of Family Structure on Child Well-Being*, Couples and Marriage Series Brief No. 3, Center for Law and Social Policy, May.

Parke, R. and Swain, D. (1975). "Infant characteristics and behaviour as elicitors of maternal and paternal responsiveness in the newborn period", Paper presented at the meeting of the *Society for Research in Child Development*, Denver, CO, April.

Pleck, J. (1997). "Paternal involvement: Levels, sources, and consequences", in M. Lamb (Ed.), *The role of the father in child development* (pp. 66-103), Third Edition, New York: John Wiley and Sons, Radin, N. Primary.

Poppenoe, D. (1996). *Life without father: Compelling new evidence that fatherhood and marriage are indispensable for the good of children and society*, Free Press, New York.

Powell, A. (2012). "Decoding keys to a healthy life", *Harvard Gazette*, 2nd February.

Project MATCH Research Group. (1997). "Matching alcoholism treatment to client heterogeneity: Project MATCH post-treatment drinking outcomes", *Journal of Studies on Alcohol*, 58: 7-29.

Project MATCH Research Group. (1998). "Matching alcoholism treatments to client heterogeneity: Project MATCH three-year drinking outcomes", *Alcoholism: Clinical and Experimental Research*, 22: 1300-1311.

Pruett, K. (1997). "How men and children affect each other's development", *Zero to Three*, 18: 3-11.

Robinson, B. (2001). *Fathering from the fast lane*, Finch Publishing.

Risch, S., Jodl, K. and Eccles, J. (2004). "Role of the father-adolescent relationship in shaping adolescents' attitudes toward divorce", *Journal of Marriage and Family*, 66: 46-58.

Rohr, R. (2005). *From Wild Man to Wise Man*, St Anthony Press, Chapters 11 and 12.

Rowe, M., Cocker, D. and Pan, B. (2004). *Gender and Parenthood: Biological and Social Scientific Perspectives*, Columbia University Press. See also: Rowe, M., Cocker, D. and Pan, B. (2004). "A comparison of fathers' and mothers' talk to toddlers in low-income families", *Social Development*, 13: 278-291.

Russell, D. (1984). "The prevalence and seriousness of incestuous abuse: stepfathers vs biological fathers", *Child Abuse and Neglect*, 8: 15-22.

Sandford, J. and Sandford, P. (2007). *Transforming the inner man*, Strang Communications Company.

Schlemon, B. (1975). *Healing Prayer*, Ave Maria Press.

Sigle-Rushton, W. and McLanahan, S. (2002), "Father absence and child well-being: A critical review", (No. 2002-20), Princeton, NJ: Centre for Research on Child Well-being.

Spear, L. (2000). "The adolescent brain and age-related behavioral manifestations", *Neuroscience and Biobehavioral Reviews*, 24: 417-463.

Solomon-fears, C., Falk, G. and Fernandes-Alcantara, A. (2013). "Child wellbeing and non-custodial fathers", *Congressional Research Service Report for Congress*. (http://fas.org/sgp/crs/misc/R41431.pdf Accessed 14th July, 2014).

Stossel, S. (2013). "What makes us happy, revisited", *The Atlantic*, May. (http://www.theatlantic.com/magazine/archive/2013/05/thanks-mom/309287/ Accessed 25th January, 2014).

Stratton, P. (2005). Report on the evidence base of systemic family therapy. (www.aft.org.uk Accessed 15th July, 2014).

Strauss, R. and Knight, J. (1999). "Influence of the home environment on the development of obesity in children", *Pediatrics*, 103: e85.

Stuart, E. (2011). "Fatherless America? A third of children now live without their dad", *Desert News*, May 22. (http://www.deseretnews.com/article/700137767/Fatherless-America-A-third-of-children-now-live-without-dad.html?pg=all Accessed 9th June, 2014).

Sweller, J., van Merrienboer, J. and Paas, F. (1998). "Cognitive architecture and instructional design", *Educational Psychology Review*, 10: 251-296.

Swinton, J. (2001). *Spirituality and mental health care*, Jessica Kingsley.

Tennant-Clark, C., Fritz, J. and Beauvais, F. (1989). "Occult participation: Its impact on adolescent development", *Adolescent*, 24: 757-772.

Tiebout, H. (1944). "Therapeutic mechanisms of Alcoholics Anonymous", *American Journal of Psychiatry*, 100: 468-473.

Thurstin, A., Alfano, A. and Nerviano, V. (1987). "The efficacy of AA attendance for aftercare of inpatient alcoholics: some follow-up data", *The International Journal of the Addictions*, 22: 1083-1090.

Timko, C. and Debenedetti, A. (2007). "A randomized controlled trial of intensive referral to 12-step self-help groups: one-year outcomes", *Drug and Alcohol Dependence*, 90: 270-279.

Timko, C., Finney, J. and Moos, R. (2005). "The 8-year course of alcohol abuse: gender differences in social context and coping", *Alcoholism: Clinical and Experimental Research*, 29: 612-621.

Tomasello, M., Kruger, A. and Ratner, H. (1993). "Cultural learning", *Behavioural and Brain Sciences*, 16: 495-552.

Townsend, N. (2002). *The Package Deal: Marriage, Work, and Fatherhood in Men's Lives*, Temple University Press.

Vaillant, G. (1977). *Adaptation to life*, Harvard University Press.

Vaillant, G. (1983). *The Natural History of Alcoholism: Causes, Patterns and Paths to Recovery*, Harvard University Press.

Vaillant, G. (2002). *Aging well*, Scribe Publications.

Vaillant, G. (2012). *Triumphs of excellence*, Belkpap Publications.

Vaillant, G. (2013). What are the secrets to a happy life? *Greater Good, The Science of a Meaningful Life*, 6th August. (http://greatergood.berkeley.edu/article/item/what_are_secrets_to_happy_life Accessed, 25th January, 2013).

Walsh, D., Hingson, R., Merrigan, D., Levenson, S., Cupples, L., Heeren, T., Coffman, G., Becker, C., Barker, T., Hamilton, S., McGuire, T. and Kelly, C. (1991). "A randomized trial of treatment options for alcohol-abusing workers", *New England Journal of Medicine*, 325: 775-782.

Weitoft, G., Hjern, A., Haglund, B. and Rosen, M. (2003). "Mortality, severe morbidity, and injury in children living with single parents in Sweden: a population-based study", *The Lancet*, 361: 289-295.

Wells, L. and Rankin, J. "Families and delinquency: A meta-analysis of the impact of broken homes", *Social Problems*, 38: 71-93.

White, W. and Laudet, A. (2006). "Life meaning as potential mediator of 12-step participation benefits on stable recovery from polysubstance use", *The College on Problems of Drug Dependence*, Vol. 22. Scottsdale, AZ.

White-Traut, R. and Watanabe, K. (2009). "Detection of salivary oxytocin levels in lactating women", *Developmental Psychobiology*, 51: 367-373.

Wilcox, W. and Kline, K. (2013). *Gender and Parenthood: Biological and Social Scientific Perspectives*, Columbia University Press.

Worthington, E. (2004). "The new science of forgiveness". (http://greatergood.berkeley.edu/article/item/the_new_science_of_forgiveness Accessed 22nd April, 2014).

Ye, Y. and Kaskutas, L. (2009). "Using propensity scores to adjust for selection bias when assessing the effectiveness of Alcoholics Anonymous in observational studies", *Drug and Alcohol Dependence*, 104: 56-64.

Yogman, M., Kindlon, D. and Earls, F. (1995). "Father involvement and cognitive/behavioral outcomes of preterm infants", *Journal of the American Academy of Child and Adolescent Psychiatry*, 34: 58-66.

Yuan, A. and Hamilton, H. (2006). "Stepfather involvement and adolescent well-being", *Journal of Family Issues*, 27: 1191-1213.

Zak, P. (2012). *The moral molecule: The source of love and prosperity*, Dutton.

Zak, P. Stanton, A. and Ahmadi, S. (2007). "Oxytocin Increases Generosity in Humans". (http://www.neuroeconomicstudies.org/images/stories/documents/ZakGenerosity.pdf Accessed 22nd April, 2014).

Zemore, S. (2007). "A role for spiritual change in the benefits of 12-step involvement", *Alcoholism: Clinical & Experimental Research*, 31: 76s–79s.

Zill, N. and Shoenborn, C. (1990). "Development, learning and social problems: Health of our nation's children", United States, 1988, National Center for Health Statistics, No. 120.

Zillman, D. (1985). "Effects of prolonged consumption of pornography", *Report prepared for the Sugeon General of the United States*. (http://profiles.nlm.nih.gov/ps/access/NNBCKV.pdf Accessed, 15th January, 1985).

Zimmerman, M., Salem, D. and Maton, K. (1995). "Family structure and psychosocial correlates among urban African-American adolescent males", *Child Development*, 66: 1598-1613.

Zimmerman, M., Salem, D. and Notaro, P. (2000). "Make room for daddy II: The positive effects of fathers' role in adolescent development", in R. Taylor and M. Wang (Eds.), *Resilience across contexts: Family, work, culture, and community* (pp. 233-253), Mahwah, NJ: Lawrence Erlbaum Associates, Inc.

Appendix I

Personal stories

Rough Diamond

In the words of the common vernacular my Dad was a "tough bastard", raised in a tough school but highly intelligent and resourceful. If you took him on physically or intellectually you did so at your peril!

He was hard drinking, hard living, serially unfaithful, violent, angry, opinionated, prejudiced, brutal and a wife beater. We lived in constant fear of him and what he might do to us or Mum.

I hated him!

He could also be charming, entertaining, was a great raconteur, generous to a fault, singer, guitar player and humourist of note. A street angel, home devil. Not to say that he pretended to be one or the other; they were just different facets of this complicated man, as I came to eventually understand.

He was Catholic school educated at Auckland Grammar, Auckland, New Zealand, by the Christian Brothers, and though a believer, it was a belief worn thin by depravation, cynicism and a tough school. Any-one seen the film, "Once We Were Warriors"? This film, with its depiction of anger, alcohol and domestic violence was our life, and reflected Dad's own history. I can't watch the film through, as it raises too many memories. The film looks at the difficulties of Maori subculture but as many know the problems dealt with cross cultural and socio-economic levels.

Shortly after his birth, Dad's mother contracted TB. In those days this meant a protracted stay in a sanatorium; in her case this was a twelve months sojourn. His father, unable to cope with a newborn baby, farmed him out to the relatives, who from all accounts generously took over his care. Unfortunately in those twelve months my grandfather had an affair that led to a permanent relationship, so he left my grandmother. Dad's mum, on leaving the sanatorium, divorced and a single mum, left the 'care' arrangements in place, and didn't take him back into her home again until she had remarried two years later, and even then, not straight away. It's not hard to imagine there were some abandonment issues on Dad's part.

The story gets worse. When Dad came back into his mother's household he was only there about a year before he was put into boarding school, at the age of five! The school was about two hundred metres from their house. Apparently Dad would climb the chapel bell tower because he could see the roof of his mother's house from there and while up there alone, would have a good cry.

Being the runt of his class he found himself the brunt of the bullies' attentions. At the age of eight he decided to do something about it. Taking himself off to the local Police and Citizens youth club he learnt how to box. When he thought himself good enough he picked the biggest bully in the class and decked him. No-one bothered him after that. Unfortunately this became his "modus operandi" for life, i.e. punch first, ask questions later. This philosophy may well have been good survival behaviour for boarding school of the 1940s/50s but not great training for family life.

Dad's other great love was rugby union. Unfortunately he would confuse the two sports of rugby and boxing which would land him in trouble particularly on the rugby field as he would never take a backward step. This probably explains that while making the school's first fifteen rugby side in his final year he was the only member of the team that was not also a school prefect.

Dad grew up being able to drink, fight, swear and seduce with the best of them. He continued with his boxing and became an amateur boxer of note with about fifty bouts, losing only two. As a result he was respected and feared by his enemies and respected and loved by his friends. If you were his friend he was generous, loyal to a fault and would defend you to the death. If you were deemed an "enemy" and took him on … he took no prisoners.

Dad's family were certainly not in the money and by mid-teens you were expected to be out working, but Dad broke the mould and continued with his secondary education. As his parents couldn't afford to keep him at school Dad would work during his holidays at his uncle's colliery humping bags of coal to pay for his own education … not only then, but would disappear during the term to work a week or two at a time to raise extra funds. On investigating these disappearances, the then headmaster on discovering the reason, waived some of the fees to keep Dad at school. Thank-you Brother who ever you were.

Not only did he finish his secondary education but he did a family first and went on to university and completed his physiotherapy training … the first of his family to complete tertiary education. Another strange facet of this man, driven to self-improvement and breaking new ground, yet partying hard and living like there was no tomorrow. His education didn't stop with his formal education; Dad read the entire encyclopaedia Britannica, cover to cover, every volume, twice. A prolific reader, he always had a pile of books on his bedside table that were at various stages of being read. His breadth of knowledge on a range of subjects was formidable. Dad was intelligent and articulate, which seems almost an oxymoron for a man who swore so much.

Enter my mother, another physio traveling through from Perth, Australia, who was on the first leg of a plan to work her way around the world. Invited by a new friend to a blind date with my father as the mystery gentleman, Mum was smitten by his charm, conversation and utterly transfixed by his colourful language. Mum came from a genteel background. On her mother's side she was related to Norwegian aristocracy while her father was a hard-working, stoic, Calvinist protestant with a moral and work ethic to match. He had risen to the rank of Lieutenant-Colonel in the Australian Army, was president of the RSL, president of the Royal Commonwealth Society, and rose to be the most senior public servant in the West Australian government ... the strongest word I ever heard my grandfather express was, "damn". Mum had never heard the words that flowed from my father's mouth, especially in combination. With Dads charm, shared profession, story-telling and attack on life, Mum was smitten.

They were married after a short engagement but things began unravelling as early as the honeymoon. Mum should have expected some problems when it turned out their honeymoon was at the same resort as Dad's rugby club wind-up ... his days were spent out drinking with his mates, staggering back to his room and when he was thoroughly drunk she had her first experiences of his post alcohol aggression. Soon after mum fell pregnant with their first child, my brother, Mike. The die was cast.

Dad proved to have little insight into family or married life – he didn't have a clue! He was a social animal and marriage and (eventually) six children failed to rein that in. He would often come home late with no explanation, drunk, or worse – the other side of drunk when inebriation was becoming aggression. He worked hard but played hard while Mum picked up the pieces in terms of home life. She was our stability and in my eyes a living saint. Dad, on the other hand, was a demon. Virtually every night would erupt into a fight with Dad extolling a list of mum's (and our) inadequacies and incompetence with language that was demeaning and destructive, using every foul word extensively and often.

We children learnt to fear him and to hate him. When we heard his car drive in we would run and hide, then listen to hear what mood he was in before we emerged from our hiding places ... was it safe?

This brings me to a pivotal night when I was seventeen. I was lying on my bed reading when a fight broke out between Mum and Dad in the kitchen. The shouting escalated, then the muffled sound of something physical going down brought my brother and me running to the confrontation. Mike got there first. When I arrived he was standing between them holding a hand up to Dad keeping him from Mum who was on the floor. Mum sat there weeping. I joined in holding Dad off – the atmosphere tense and menacing. Dad angry, eyes wide with an almost glazed look in his eyes stormed off to his cave while we helped Mum up and comforted her.

When the dust had settled I returned to my room devastated that another such event had occurred. I wept with anger, despair, grief and frustration. I remember almost shaking my fist at God and saying, "If you're real then you better make yourself known to me now because if you're not this whole thing (life) is a waste of time."

I felt so low, so desperate I just wanted to find the nearest bridge and jump off. Then something strange happened. I sensed someone had entered my room and I turned to shout at them to get out as I thought it was one of my siblings and I was embarrassed by my tears and emotional state ... but no-one was there! I went back to my weeping and wailing but was interrupted by the same sense that someone was entering my room. I turned again but with the same result ... no-one there.

Standing there bemused I had the incredible experience of feeling a presence in the room with me. I felt suddenly peaceful and calm, if a little confused. I've described the experience as not like seeing light but feeling light. The experience lasted for about ten minutes then the sense of the presence slowly faded, leaving me incredulous but buoyed. I realized something amazing – God had answered my desperate prayer. I recognised two important things instantly:

1) God was real!
2) He cared enough about me to make a direct intervention into my life at the bequest of my prayer ... this was not a distant God but a God who wanted a personal relationship. These conclusions were reinforced the next morning.

I awoke the next day to doubts. Had I really experienced God's healing presence or was it all a psychological illusion that I had created because my need was so great? Had my mind produced it to quiet my trauma? As I was contemplating this I was sitting at the kitchen table munching on my morning bowl of cornflakes when I noticed a small religious magazine called 'The Messenger' that my Mother used to get. I had never read it before but I started leafing through it as I ate. I began reading the story of a French Bishop describing his own conversion experience. It went something like this.

The Bishop's family had fled Russia after the revolution and settled in France. His family were religious but as a young man the Bishop abandoned his faith and became the young radical. Indeed, on attending the Sorbonne University he became a leader of the anarchy movement. This aggressive and radical view of life failed to bring peace or happiness, just bitterness and hate. One day while sitting in the university library a sense of emptiness and lack of purpose overwhelmed him and he decided to end it all. With every intention of leaving the library, finding a gun and blowing his brains out, he looked up and in the shelves opposite saw a Bible sitting there. It was then he prayed, "God if you're real, make yourself known to me now otherwise this life is a waste of time."

I recognised immediately the similarity to the prayer I had blurted out the day before. He pulled the Bible from the shelf and sat down at the table and started reading the New Testament. A few moments into his reading he looked up sensing someone had sat at his table, but no-one was there! He went back to his reading only to have an even stronger sense of someone joining him at the library table, looking up again he saw … no-one! As he sat there he became aware of a presence with him, unseen but felt. He then went on to describe exactly the experience I had the day before, the sense of peace and joy invaded his spirit.

He left that library a different man, convinced of God's reality and his love of him personally, eventually becoming a Catholic priest and ultimately an Archbishop.

I finished the story and sat there stunned. Looking to the heavens I said, "OK, I get it! The experience was real." That experience changed the colour of my life. It set me on a path of discovery, deepening my knowledge of, and love for God and the Church. This experience of my Heavenly Father's love led me eventually to healing and restoring my earthly father's relationship.

My journey from there led me to discover the Catholic Charismatic Renewal where I found people who experienced and expected to have a personal relationship with God, whose faith was real, deep and active with vibrant worship services, miraculous manifestations and powerful prayer lives. It was while attending these prayer meetings that I had the growing realisation that I needed to forgive my father for all his faults, failings and foibles. In my new found spiritual life I embraced the concept quickly … the reality of forgiving was a little more challenging.

A few months into attending these prayer meetings I was deep in prayer with a gentleman one night when he suddenly opened his eyes, looked at me and said, "I just had a strong sense that The Lord wants you to go home and tell your Father that you love him."

I was shaken, my heart went cold, a pit of fear welled up in my stomach … this was going too far … I wasn't ready … God was being unreasonable. All these thoughts and more stirred in me.

As I drove home that night I wrestled with the concept, concluding that it was too difficult, impossible for me at the moment. Yet when I got home and Dad happened to open the front door to let me in, as he stood there I blurted out, "I love you Dad!" These words had never escaped my lips before. We stood looking at each other for an awkward moment then Dad replied, "That's good, I was wondering there for a while." Then the moment was passed. Dad went off to watch more telly and I wandered off into my room elated. For all its anticlimax I knew that our relationship was now different, it was never to be the same. It was irrevocably changed for the better.

It continued to develop and improve over the next decade. He mellowed, we cut him a bit of slack. Meanwhile the relationship with God, my heavenly Father, also blossomed. I must confess to relating to the person of Jesus much better than that of the Father in my early spiritual walk. I was still influenced by my past and my Catholic upbringing where I had experienced (rightly or wrongly) the image of God as a distant, casual observer of our lives, a bearded austere judge, up there beyond the clouds. This image was dealt a severe blow when my wife and I visited Israel in 2000. We were having dinner in the hotel restaurant on a Friday evening (beginning of the Jewish Sabbath) and noted an orthodox Jewish family setting up for their Sabbath meal. A little boy about three ran around the table to his father crying out, "Abba, Abba" and leapt into his Father's lap where he snuggled into his father's embrace. This is the equivalent of saying, "Daddy, Daddy". I remembered the scripture from Romans 8:15, "… instead you have received the spirit of God's adopted children by which we call out, 'Abba Father'."

I had an "Ah Ha" moment and realised the intimacy of the relationship that God wanted with us. After this incident I started using the word 'Daddy' in my prayer … this felt very uncomfortable. I felt I was being too familiar and even to this day I can get coy saying those words in prayer but I'm getting there.

Meanwhile if I can return to my father's story, our relationship improved to the point where I joined his physiotherapy practice in 1989 and for two years we worked together more or less congenially. Late in 1990 he was diagnosed with liver cancer and a very difficult twelve months ensued. Major surgery and chemotherapy followed, his pain and discomfort was enormous, but his courage was obvious. His growing reliance on Mum was great and his approaching death encouraged further reconciliation with the family.

Towards the end of that year, as hard as it had been, he told my mother that it had been the best year of his life. We are a society that avoids suffering at all cost, but here I could see suffering had a purpose … a salvific one.

He came back to the Church and received the sacraments again, something he had not done for many years (mostly out of guilt after being caught in an extramarital affair and a personal protest at the loss of the Latin Mass … as I said he was a complicated man).

As his time drew near he became weaker, yet also more gentle and open. His time with my two young children born at the time, was beautiful to watch, and so different from my own upbringing. The relationship with my mother was also interesting to watch as Dad relied more and more on her care. They grew closer and more intimate, my mother's capacity for forgiveness, her patience, love and care for Dad were extraordinary in view of his long term treatment of her. She was an amazing woman.

Dad died in the early hours of the morning at Bethesda hospital in late August, 1991. The evening before, my brother, Mike, and I were at his bedside. He lay there to all intents and purposes, comatose! My brother and I had been singing gentle worship songs from the early renewal days. I started to feel sorry for Dad. He loved music, especially the crooners, Crosby, Sinatra, Dean Martin, etc. and here he was a captured audience with us getting all religious on him. So I thought I would balance things up by singing a bit of Bing, 'White Christmas', to be exact. I started to sing and Dad's eyes flashed open and he forcefully exclaimed, "No!" Mike and I were taken aback, we hadn't thought him conscious. We looked at each other dumbfounded. I looked back at Dad and asked:

"Do you want us to continue singing Christian songs, Dad?"
He replied immediately.
"Yes", he said clearly and emphatically.

We continued and he settled back, closed his eyes, and lay there peacefully once more. He passed away a few hours later … the Prodigal Son on his journey home.

What a turnaround, this man that I had hated and wished dead, I had grown to love and forgive and now miss. I can only put this down to the healing action of my God made available when I opened up my life to his grace and mercy and made the decision to forgive. When I was able as an adult to look past my own pain and brokenness and see the 'damaged goods' that was my father, I could look with compassion and understanding on his life and be amazed at what he accomplished.

I have largely avoided the sins of my father in my own life and enjoy a wonderful marriage and appear to have six well adjusted (so far) children, a great job, great friends, a great life, but I am not perfect by any means and have made my share of mistakes. I know my journey is still unfolding but it would have been so much tougher and confused if not for the experience of a loving God who filled in the holes left in my heart from my poor relationship with Dad, yet at the same time restored to me my earthly father.

Greg Diamond

Voyage without my father

In the 1960s the English lawyer turned playwright, John Mortimer, wrote a play entitled, "Voyage around my Father", about his life growing up with his blind, irascible and eccentric father, for whom he had a difficult but enduring love. If I were to write a play about my experience of my father, I would have to call it, "Voyage without my Father". This year, on May 5th, 2014, I am 58 years old. This year, on May 31st, my father has been dead 50 years. So this year marks 50 years of missing my Dad. 50 years of an absence, which feels, at times, as strong as a presence. This absence is not merely emptiness or a vacuum, as I have memories, others' memories and stories, imagination, brief glimpses from the past that I hold close to my heart. And I have the father of my dreams and prayers to sustain me.

What can I write about my father and his fatherhood, when I have experienced only eight years of my father, and that was 50 years ago? I will write about my memories. I will write about my hopes. I will write about my fears. I will write about my being a father. I will write about my loss and his absence and what that means to me now. What I do not want to do is write academically or theoretically or abstractly. I don't want to preach or sermonise. This is not a 'self-help' or 'how to' article. I don't want to write this at a safe distance. I want to write about my personal experience and my emotions around him honestly and openly. However, I do not want my story to be sentimental or maudlin. I believe, as Carl Rogers did, that what is most personal is most general. So maybe you will understand yourself or someone else from my voyage without my father.

My older memories of him are blurry and vague. I remember driving, before I started school, with him on his trips to farmers and businesses in the country. Just him and me in the front seat of the car through the bush. I remember him lighting sky rockets, and roman candles, and Catherine wheels around the bonfire on cracker night. I remember fishing and crabbing with him at Hervey Bay. I remember him taking up the collection at Sunday Mass. Then the memories become sharper, more defined with his dying. His death was a turning point, a watershed, a defining event in my life and in my development. In some ways it felt like the end of my childhood. I never got to say goodbye to him or to it.

On my 8th birthday, I was summoned into his room to his sickbed, and the man I had remembered as tall and strongly built, had shrivelled to a leathery skeletal stranger who handed me a rugby league football for my birthday present. I don't remember if he actually could speak to me. I said 'Thank-you' and left as quickly as I could. I remember feeling afraid and confused. No one forewarned me. I didn't recognise him and that was the last time I saw him alive. Four weeks later, I went to his requiem Mass at St Stephen's Cathedral and I remember his coffin and the grey-gloved funeral director and pall bearers and the sheer exhaustion of holding back tears for so long and then drowning in the perfumey powdery sympathy of his sisters, my aunts and so many unknown mourners.

Regretfully, I never went to his burial. To this day, I wish that I had. Maybe I would have stopped hoping he might return if I had witnessed the finality of his interment. For children then, in my family, were shielded from the point blank barrel of life by not being present. At least that was the theory. In reality, nothing could be further from the truth. My mother was dealing with her own grief; who had the time or skill to help an eight-year-old boy deal with his?

I remember a couple of years after my father's death, when we had moved to Brisbane, and I began grade 5 at an all boys' school, at the start of the year a teacher who I am sure meant well, but on reflection displayed a complete lack of sense, sensitivity and awareness of his class asked each boy, one by one, to stand and tell the class what his father's occupation was. Why this was relevant or how this was educational, I do not know. I was up the front and the announcements began up the back. I was so anxious in waiting my turn I broke into a cold sweat. Internally I was frantically deciding whether I would tell the truth or tell the teacher what my Dad did before he died, just to save face. One by one the boys stood and listed the various occupations: 'policeman', 'cab driver', 'bank manager', 'truck driver', 'invalid', 'unemployed fisherman', 'butcher', 'accountant', 'builder'. All sounded so important, so special. …… Then me – finally – 'my Dad's dead, Sir'. His uncomfortable silence. My public humiliation. My vulnerability laid bare for all to pity. I sat down not knowing where to look, hoping that the floor would swallow me up. OK, now it was news – I was different. You had a Dad with important sounding work, a bread-winner, a hero, someone to boast about. Not me. Not the same as you or you, who were unscathed by the terrible mystery of death. I felt incredibly inferior, incredibly alone, and incredibly isolated.

A father matters more than he can know. No 10-year-old boy should feel like that. I will never forget that class or the effect that an ignorant teacher can have on a boy. On the positive side, I now always keep a wary eye out for boys in my classes who do not have fathers who are present in their lives. I know how it feels. I know what a powerful effect a kind and compassionate male teacher can have on a boy too.

I remember at 14, waking with a start during the night, seeing what I thought was the vague outline of a man, at the foot of my bed – It was in fact a hanging coat on the back of the door to my bedroom – thinking it was him, and for a moment believing his death was just a bad dream and here he was alive and real, and the experience of his death was just an illusion. And here he was to bring me comfort, protection, manhood, and love. I remember praying a prayer over and over in my mind – "Please let it be him. Please let it be him. Please let it be him." And then that awful truth dropped like a heavy stone into a still pond – that he was dead and that he was not returning, that I was still alone, that I did not have him anymore, and that was that. And to personalise the words of Milton's poem: "I woke – he fled – and day brought back my night".

During my adolescence, I missed him most, I think. There was no shield, no buffer, no safety net, no compass, no guiding hand, no shoulder, no sounding board, and I could not share this with anyone. This is not to deny or discount the significance of my mother, who was a rock, but she was not my father. A mother can certainly talk to her son about becoming a good man, but a father can actually model for his son what it means, especially without words, – and that witness is so powerful. So I felt I was always cutting my own track through the jungle of my teenage years, searching for the way to manhood. There was no one leading me by the hand through the dangers and pitfalls of this journey. It was trial and error, being hyper-vigilant, looking for clues and cues from other young men whose fathers, I presumed, showed them the way. This ordeal went unspoken, unacknowledged. It was just get on with it. This is your lot, your life. Deal with it. You are not the only one who has ever lost a father. But there was a pain and sadness that lingered there in the corner of my life, no matter how much I tried to be brave.

Always there – the shadow, the silhouette, the outline of my grief. And I never felt safe enough to talk about it with anyone, and anyhow, no one ever broached the issue. I am not sure if I could have talked about it even if they did.

I remember when there were annual Father and Son events at my school. Well-meaning friends or at least their kind and considerate Dads would ask me if I wanted to join them. Absolutely and categorically, NOT. I was not going to be the target of someone's pity. I was not going to parade my fatherlessness before every father and son at my school. That had been done before by that insensitive teacher. No thank you, not this time. If these are the cards that life had dealt me, then I wasn't going to pretend otherwise. Deeper inside myself, though, I thought what I would have given to have gone to a Father and Son event with my Dad. When I saw other boys' fathers watching them play footie, what I wouldn't have given to have him on the sideline watching me tackle hard and low. What I wouldn't have given to hear his words of encouragement and excitement. What I wouldn't have given for my Dad to be crazy about me, his boy. That is what the loss of my father meant to me, as a schoolboy, and I didn't talk about that with anyone.

Not having my Dad present in my life, not seeing him relating to my Mum, or parenting my sisters, meant I did not have a lived experience of seeing husband and wife live and love together. I grew up as the only male in an all-female family – my mother and five sisters. So now for me being the father of a 12-year-old son and a nine-year-old daughter has been a journey of discovery, not just discovering who they are, but discovering who I am through them, with them, and for them. My identity has changed because of them.

My experience of fatherhood has been a revelation – a gift and a task. There have been many moments of grace, where it was like my son and my daughter at different times have shown me in their own ways what they needed in a Dad. They showed me how to be a Dad! I will recount two of these moments of grace. I remember feeding my son his bottle as a toddler. It was late into the night and his crying had woken me up. It was my turn for feeding and I wandered bleary eyed into the room where he sat with his hands on the bars of his cot – looking like a mini prisoner in his striped pyjamas. He lay down as I settled next to the cot and I held the bottle for him as he sucked away. At one point, in his utter contentment, his eyes met mine, and strangely we gazed at each other for what seemed like minutes. I didn't avert my gaze and neither did he. It was a beautiful and unnerving moment. I felt like he was peering into my soul, peering into his future with me. How was I going to measure up as his Dad?

The Irish have a phrase 'thin spaces' – it is when the veil between the divine and the human is almost lifted and you sense the depth and holiness of the Other in that space and time. This was one of those moments for me.

With my daughter, I have also experienced that 'thin space'. Recently, walking with her, on a nightly walk with our little dog, she put her arm around my waist as we were chatting away. I couldn't wait to tell my wife about it when we got home – that my nine-year-old daughter, so unselfconsciously, so affectionately, put her arm around her Dad. It was such a small gesture but it was so powerful for me that my eyes moistened with love and joy.

As a Dad, I receive so much from my children, so many indications and signs about what they want me to be for them. So as a Dad, I watch and I listen to them. That is not always easy in the busyness of daily work and family life. But the difference just 'being there' makes in behaviour, communication, and family life, when I attend to them is profound.

Conclusion

Every now and then the absence of my father pierces my day to day activities. Recently, talking to a neighbour who is 10 years younger than me, I mentioned proudly that I had just purchased a new expensive lawn mower and I was waxing lyrical about this 4 stroke's capabilities, and doing some mechanical chest beating. He then responded with: "I've still got the mower that my father bought me when my wife and I moved into our first home". That statement stopped me in my tracks and it hit home that I have yet another loss of not having my father into my adult years. I know that sounds strange, but the reality of my journey without my father cut deep that day.

I remember a statement of one of my counselling clients, as he left my office to visit his elderly father – "a son is never too old to hang out with his Dad'. I miss being able to have that experience. The reality is that I cannot evade or avoid the fact that my father is dead. His presence through his absence is a steady reminder of the importance of my father still. I would be naive to think that he doesn't matter now.

Certainly, for all of us sons, fathers, present or absent, compassionate or callous, engaged or disengaged, matter much more than we realise, for the whole of our lives, and on to our children's lives too. For me, that means that I will never discount my role as father, or trivialise my power for good in my own children's lives. I am father to them forever. In the words of Shakespeare, 'it is a wise man who knows his own children'.

I wonder if I asked you to write a story or book about your experience of growing up with your father what would you call it? What would be the main themes? What would be the emotions expressed? What would be the ending? What would you be thankful for? What would you have desired but never got? I wonder too if my son ever writes the story of me, his father, what would he call it? What would your son write about you?

Brian Sullivan, March 2014.

A wife and mother's perspective

At the time of writing these words Robert and I (Alicia) had just celebrated our 31st wedding anniversary. This caused me to reflect on the past years and how happy I am in my relationship with Robert now and in past times how unhappy I had been. I asked myself at the hardest times, "what made me stay in the marriage and why did I not just throw in the towel?" After all I know that the later would have been the easier option. I cringe when I think that I could have even considered the latter option, as now I could not see myself with any other person.

I think now there is more balance in our relationship and shared responsibilities. I feel loved, valued, important and cared for. I know Robert will always choose me first. This however, has not always been the case. Academic, John Gottman, found in a 1999 newlywed study that sixty-seven percent of couples undertook a precipitous drop in marital satisfaction upon the arrival of their first child. I felt in this category. I wanted to be in the other 33 precent, but this took years to achieve.

As time progressed, it seemed that we both had separate lives. Robert was building his business and was a leader in the church community we belonged to and I was a mother at home with four children. I did not have enough self-confidence to say to Robert, "Hey I am unhappy". I did not even know what words to say and what would happen if he yelled at me. So I spent years in a passive aggressive state, becoming more and more angry on the inside. I would stonewall Robert, rather than confronting him. I would disengage, I would avoid a fight, but on the other hand I was avoiding our marriage.

In my eyes Robert was doing good work and providing for our family. I felt selfish if I complained and I was overwhelmed enough to stonewall; it seemed my only option. What I did not realise at the time was that the more space Robert took to grow himself, the less I was growing in myself. This was a huge imbalance in our relationship, which created tension and anxiety between us. This tension and anxiety spread out toward the children, which generated more tension and anxiety. I was emotionally lonely.

I knew things needed to change but did not know where to start. This is where God and his infinite wisdom cared enough to enter our marriage and help us set it back on the right path. As a counsellor I see couples stuck, and I work with the one who is most able to change. God as our counsellor decided to work in Robert. Through prayer and a deeper relationship with Jesus, I noticed over time Robert was changing; becoming less absorbed with himself and his work in the business world and the community. He trusted God with these things, which meant he could let go of some control he had on his world. This meant that he had more energy for the children and me. It took one person to change and set the ball rolling. I am much happier and content now.

No longer did Robert need to borrow time, energy and space from the family to prop himself up. This renewed balance meant that I had space to grow myself and change. I am now following my passion and doing what I was made to do. Becoming more of a real self and changing. I know it will be a life long journey for me. I do thank God for his goodness and for Robert listening to God, without this our marriage and my life would be very different.

Alicia Falzon

Appendix II

Supporting evidence

AII.1 Examining the evidence for the effectiveness of Alcoholics Anonymous

This appendix summarises the review of the evidence for AA's effectiveness which was provided in (Kaskutas, 2009). That review looked at the totality of the available evidence, avoiding the trap of simply focussing on evidence compiled from one narrow domain of testing.

The review in (Kaskutas, 2009) used a broad framework for evaluating evidentiary causality. This framework was first established in the context of research on the health effects of smoking. In the case of smoking it would have been unethical to test for causality with conventional randomised controlled trials (RCTs) in which smokers were randomised to either a smoking or non-smoking condition. A broad framework for testing was therefore devised. Similarly, it is often ethically problematical or practically awkward to randomise subjects to either an AA or non-AA intervention. A small number of studies have done this kind of randomisation, but they have often been riddled with practical problems and serious design flaws.

The broad framework for evaluating causality involves testing in six different areas:

1. Strength of effect.
2. Dose-response relationship.
3. Consistency of association.
4. Predictability of effects.
5. Coherence with existing knowledge.
6. Specificity.

In Categories 1, 2, 3, 4 and 5 the evidence in favour of AA effectiveness is very strong. In Category 6 the evidence is weakest and this is not entirely surprising. Specificity is usually established with RCTs and, as already mentioned, it is very challenging to devise reliable RCTs for testing AA's effectiveness. Details of the findings in the six categories are provided below.

Strength of effect

The effect being considered here is the effect of AA participation on abstinence form alcohol. If AA is effective, one would expect AA participants to be more likely to abstain from alcohol than non-participants in AA. This is precisely what research has found. Rates of abstinence are about twice as high among those who have attended a Twelve Step program after treatment for alcoholism (Ouimette er al, 1998; Thurstin et al, 1987).

Dose response relationship

What is tested here is whether higher levels of attendance at AA correspond to higher levels of abstinence. Tests have actually shown that abstinence rates increase with various different measures of attendance. Specifically, abstinence increases with (Moos and Moos, 2006):

i) the number of AA meetings attended,

ii) the frequency of meetings attended and

iii) the duration of AA attendance.

Consistency of association

The association between AA participation and abstinence has been found in numerous studies. In addition to the ones mentioned in the two previous categories, supporting studies have been done by Timko, Dawson and co-workers (Dawson et al, 2006; Timko et al, 2000). In the study by Timko et al, it was found that about 50% of AA participants were abstinent after three and eight years, whereas only about 20% of non-AA participants were abstinent after the same period.

In the investigation by Dawson et al, it was found that individuals with lifetime drinking problems who attended AA were more likely to be abstinent than those who did not attend AA or any other treatment.

Predictability of effects

To establish causality one has to show that the cause precedes the effect. For AA research one has to show that abstinence occurred after attendance at AA and not the other way round. This can be done by examining evidence of the effect after the intervention has ceased.

Two key studies have affirmed the predictability of AA's effectiveness – a study by Moos (Moos and Moos, 2006) and a study known as 'Project Match' (Connors et al, 2001). The study in (Moos and Moos, 2006) followed a cohort of problem drinkers who had not previously been treated over a period of 16 years. Abstinence in years 8-16 was found to be significantly correlated with AA participation in years 2-3 and 4-8. Similarly, Project Match found that AA participation in months 1-6 predicted abstinence in months 7-12.

Coherence with existing knowledge

The question addressed for this criterion is: "Does AA work in a fashion which is consistent with established theoretical understanding of health behaviour and behavioural change?"

Contemporary psychodynamic theory suggests that alcoholics tend to have a narcissistic personality and a strong sense of omnipotence. They also tend to have difficulty expressing their feelings and self-regulating their behaviour (Khantzian and Mack, 1989; Tiebout, 1944). The first step of AA prompts participants to acknowledge their powerlessness. This directly addresses the misguided sense of omnipotence. Steps 2 and 3 exhort participants to embrace the help available from a higher power, which is at least partially manifested in the AA meeting as the support group. This helps to improve self-governance. Steps 4-10 encourage people to see how their behaviour affects others and to begin treating others better. This mitigates narcissistic tendencies. Step 11 engenders a sense of meaning and purpose in life, while Step 12 directs them to shift the focus away from themselves and to reach out and help others.

The AA fellowship also provides a venue where people can talk about feelings and about overcoming struggles. Typically, more experienced members share their stories with newcomers and so provide concrete examples of how to express feelings and self-regulate behaviour. The 'one day at a time' philosophy also assists with the ability to self-regulate.

Contemporary social learning theory also supports the rationale behind the AA method. That theory suggests that a large part of the problem for alcoholics derives from social influences and from the way they socially learn (Bandura, 1971; Freeman, 1995; Lave and Wenger, 1991). If a person's friends all drink then they will tend to be strongly influenced to drink in order to fit in. They will also tend to imbibe the practices and behaviours of their drinking friends. They will therefore have little motivation to stop drinking and they will not have learned how to abstain. The AA approach addresses these issues very directly. AA participants spend more time with other AA members who do not drink and who provide role modelling on how to abstain and avoid relapsing.

Many studies have lent support to the above contentions. These studies have shown that the positive association between AA participation and abstinence is mediated by such things as:

i) having fewer pro-drinking influences (Kaskutas et al, 2002),

ii) having more friends and better friendship networks (Humphreys et al, 1999; Timko et al, 2005),

iii) having AA friends supportive of abstinence (Bond et al, 2003),

iv) improved self-efficacy (Morgenstern, 1997),

v) improved coping and relapse prevention skills (Timko et al, 2005; Humphreys et al, 1999),

vi) having a greater sense of meaning in life (White et al, 2006),

vii) being more motivated to abstain (Kelly et al, 2002),

viii) changed religious beliefs and spirituality (Zenmore, 2007).

Specificity

This criterion seeks to prove that the effect (abstinence) is specifically due to the intervention (AA participation) and not to any other cause. Evidence for this criterion is usually acquired by using RCTs in which all variables are controlled except for the variable under test. The design of well controlled RCTs for testing AA effectiveness is difficult from both an ethical and practical perspective. Nonetheless a number of studies have been attempted, as described below.

Kaskutas reported that of the four key conventional RCTs used to evaluate AA's effectiveness, two produced a positive finding, one produced a null finding, and one produced a negative finding (Kaskutas, 2009). The first positive finding came from Project Match, which randomised patients to AA, Cognitive Behaviour Therapy (CBT) or Motivational Enhancement Therapy (Project Match, 1997; Project Match, 1998). This study found that the outpatients in this study were significantly more likely to be abstinent after one year and four years if they had been randomised to AA. There was no difference in abstinence rates among the three groups for aftercare patients, although this may well be because of a deficiency in the study design. Many of the patients in aftercare actually participated in AA as well as the other interventions. Thus, AA was effectively being compared with AA plus another treatment. Participation in AA also reliably predicted abstinence at a later date (for both outpatient and aftercare patients).

The second positive finding came from a study of Veterans'

Administration (VA) patients, who were randomised either to a standard AA intervention or to an intensive AA intervention. Abstinence rates were found to be significantly higher in the intensive AA intervention at the six month and 12 month follow ups (Timko and Debenedetti, 2007).

The null finding on AA effectiveness came from a court ordered intervention in which patients were randomised into one of three groups (Brandsma et al, 1980). The first group was assigned to one on one therapy sessions with lay individuals, the second was assigned to a control group which could seek any treatment they wished (including no treatment) and the third group was assigned to participate in a weekly AA-like meeting run by the study's investigators (and as such was not an authentic AA meeting). This study found at the three month follow-up that there was more binge drinking among those who participated in the AA-like meetings (2.37 binges per month) than among those who were assigned to the lay therapy (0.26 binges per month) or the control group (0.56 binges per month). This was found to be only a short-term effect, however. At the 1 year follow-up binge rates and abstinence rates were similar across the three different groups.

The study which produced a negative finding for AA effectiveness randomised patients undergoing compulsory court ordered treatment into AA participation, hospital inpatient treatment and treatment from the provider of their choice (Walsh et al, 1991). Many patients in the hospital inpatient cohort, however, actually attended AA meetings as well as hospital inpatient care. AA was therefore being compared (for many patients) with AA plus another treatment. The study neglected to account for this confounding factor. In light of this design flaw it is not surprising that the study found that those in the hospital inpatient group were about twice as likely to be abstinent as those in the AA group and the choice group.

Given the difficulties in designing rigorous RCTs, some researchers have attempted to use multivariate statistical association studies to parse out the confounding factors from observational data. A key confounding factor in AA studies is the motivation of a drinker to change. Does AA participation cause people to abstain, or do those who are motivated to change tend to go to AA? A number of multivariate statistical association studies have tried to account for the confounding factors. The results are summarised below.

One study assessed people's propensity to go to AA with a 'Propensity Scores' measure and then used these scores to disentangle the effect of a person's propensity to go to AA from the observational studies (Ye and Kaskutas, 2009). After doing so it was found that, among those with a high propensity to attend AA, the impact of AA was minimal. For those with low propensity to attend, however, the effect of AA was very significant – the odds ratio for abstinence was found to range between 2.7 and 6.9.

A second study also adjusted for motivation to attend AA and found that those who were more heavily involved in AA after 1 year had fewer drinking problems at the two year follow up interview (McKellar et al, 2003).

A third study adjusted for availability of AA meetings in one's community and the ability to drive to the meeting. After this adjustment the odds ratio for the impact of AA on abstinence reduced from 3.69 (statistically significant) to 1.67 (statistically insignificant) (Fortney et al, 1998).

A fourth study adjusted for perceived seriousness of drinking and a coping style oriented towards information seeking solutions. After these adjustments the positive impact of AA on heavy drinking was found to increase greatly, doubling in magnitude (Humphreys et al, 1996).

Overall conclusions

The evidence in support of AA's effectiveness is very strong in five out of the six categories used for establishing causality. In the sixth category (specificity) it has proved very challenging to acquire reliable evidence.

Many of the studies in this category are beset by major design flaws. One interesting study in this category has found that AA tends to be very effective for those with low levels of motivation, but relatively inconsequential for those who are already highly motivated. More testing needs to be done to ascertain whether or not this finding can be replicated consistently.

Some reviews have evaluated AAs effectiveness by focussing heavily on the category of specificity (Ferri et al, 2006). Not surprisingly, they conclude that there is insufficient evidence to verify the effectiveness of AA. This is a highly questionable approach, however. It is important to look at the totality of evidence across all six categories, five of which strongly support the positive effect of AA.

AII.2 Risk rates for youth incarceration as a function of family type

Family type	Odds ratio – youth incarceration
Intact mother-father	1
Mother only	2.17
Father only	1.12
Mother-stepfather	2.70
Father-stepmother	3.86
Relatives-other	3.12

Table A2.1. Odds ratios for youth incarceration vs family type. The higher the odds ratio, the higher is the likelihood of incarceration (from Harper and McLanahan, 2004).

AII.3 Influence of parents on children's spiritual engagement

Religious practice of the father	Religious practice of the mother	% of children who become regular as adults	% of children who become irregular as adults	% of children who do not practise as adults
Regular	Regular	32.8	41.4	25.8
Regular	Irregular	37.7	37.6	24.7
Regular	Non-practising	44.2	22.4	33.4
Irregular	Regular	3.4	58.6	38.0
Irregular	Irregular	7.8	60.8	31.4
Irregular	Non-practising	25.4	22.8	51.8
Non-practising	Regular	1.5	37.4	61.1
Non-practising	Irregular	2.3	37.8	59.9
Non-practising	Non-practising	4.6	14.7	80.7

Table A2.2. Religious practice as a function of the example set by parents (from (Fertfam, 2000)).

Appendix III

A selection of resources

Books

Healing and restoration

Transforming the inner man, by John Loren Sandford and Paula Sandford. Charisma House, 2007.

Letting Go Of Your Past: Take Control of Your Future by Addressing the Habits, Hurts, and Attitudes that Remain from Previous Relationships, by John Loren Sandford and Paula Sandford. Charisma House, 2013.

Blessing or curse: you can choose, by Derek Prince. Chosen, 1990.

Healing the family tree, by Kenneth McCall. SPOK Publishing, 2013.

Turning 'lemons into lemonade'

Prison to praise, by Merlin Carothers. Carothers Publishing, 1970.

Power in praise, by Merlin Carothers. Carothers Publishing, 1980.

Bringing heaven into hell, by Merlin Carothers. Carothers Publishing, 1984.

Fathers, fatherhood and men's growth

Fathering from the fast lane, by Bruce Robinson. Finch Publishing, 2001.

Sons of the Father, by Gordon Dalbey. Tyndale House Publishing, 1996.

Healing the Masculine Soul, by Gordon Dalbey. W Publishing Group, 1991.

Wild at heart, by John Eldridge. Thomas Nelson, 2002.

Waking the Dead, by John Eldridge. Thomas Nelson, 2003.

Fathered by God, by John Eldridge. Thomas Nelson, 2009.

From wild man to wise man, by Richard Rohr. St. Anthony Messenger Press, 2005.

Every blokes a Champion, by Ian Watson. Watto Books, 2012.

Helping children to become sexually responsible adults

As I have loved you, by Gerard O'Shea. Connor Court, 2011.

Counselling for restoring lives broken due to childhood depravation

Australia - http://www.elijahhouse.com.au/

Austria - www.elijahhouse.at

Finland - www.elijah.fi

Japan - www.ehj.jp

Malaysia - www.elijahhouse.com.my

New Zealand - www.elijahhouse.org.nz

Philippines - www.elijahhousephil.org

South Africa - www.elijahsa.za.org

Taiwan - www.elijahhousetw.org

USA - www.elijahhouse.org

Phone (Australia): 07 5492 8588

Fax (Australia): 07 5492 8599

Email (Australia): info@elijahhouse.com.au

Videos

Hugh Clark story //vimeo.com/16491186

*men*ALIVE videos

www.menalive.org.au/resources/menalive-video/

Web-sites for father's support groups

www.menalive.org.au/

www.fatherhood.org.au

www.fathersonline.org

www.abbafather.com

www.allprodad.com/

www.dads4kids.org.au

www.fatheringadventures.com.au

www.bettermen.com.au

www.careforcelifekeys.org

www.shednight.com

Support for overcoming addictions

Alcohol

www.aa.org.au/

Pornography

www.saoz.net

www.covenanteyes.com

www.guiltypleasure.tv

Drugs

www.na.org.au

Mental health issues

www.grow.net.au/

Courses for developing healthy fatherhood

"Good to Great". www.dads4kids.org.au

"Valiant Man". www.careforcelifekeys.org

Courses for fathers and their teenage sons

Growing Good Men.

www.menalive.org.au/events/growing-good-men/

Personal stories and blog

www.menalive.org.au/fatherfactor

Index

AA 23, 109, 118, 165-72
abandonment 59-60, 72, 148
absenteeism 10, 56
abstinence 166
abuse 26, 33, 47, 55-8, 65, 81, 97, 100, 108-9, 111, 124, 126
addiction 2
addiction factor 2, 22, 130
adolescence 49, 51, 129, 159
adoptive parents 89
affectionate touch 30
ageing 26
alcohol 2, 22, 26, 56-8, 112, 121, 124, 126, 147, 150, 166
Alcoholics Anonymous 23, 74, 112, 165
alcoholism 22, 23, 62, 73, 112, 118, 126, 166
anger 7, 73, 79, 105, 118, 147, 151
anxiety 43-4, 84, 87, 163
Arizona 44
asthma 46
authoritative parenting 33-4, 47, 51

Barro, Robert 41
behaviour 34, 43, 46, 49, 52, 59-60, 62-3, 67, 71, 81, 83-4, 86, 90, 102, 113-4, 124, 125, 148, 161, 167-8
Bell, Alexander Graham 20

biological parents 9, 76, 89, 95
blue ray DVD 8
body shape 27-8
Boston 24
brain cells 27
brain damage 31, 94
brain maps 120
breast-feeding 30
burden bearing 123, 125

California 24
Cambridge University 108
Camille, Godfrey Minot 69
cancer 44, 49, 51, 57, 154
CASA 108
catastrophising 84
causality 167
CBT 83, 84, 87-8, 169
Challenger Space Shuttle 41
charity 115
child support 33, 101
child-bearing 11
church attendance 106
Cognitive Behaviour Therapy 83, 169
coherence with existing knowledge 165
communication device 31
community 30, 49, 72, 82, 99, 110, 115, 118, 127, 130, 132, 163-4, 171
conference trips 92

conflict 22, 57, 102-3, 105, 115
consistency of association 165
conviction mechanism 113, 118-9, 127, 130
co-parenting environment 102
creativity 68, 114, 123
criminal acts 11
critical period 34, 71
Cruz, Nicky 110

dancing 30
daughters 5, 8, 9, 59-61, 63, 66-7, 89-90, 99, 116
de Boer, Mike 97
de Maupassant, Guy 121
deliberate practice 37-8, 40, 51
dementia 4, 21
demographic trends 16
depression 22
destiny 2, 7, 14, 60
discipline 3, 33, 38, 51, 66, 80, 101, 105
disrespect 80
divorce rates 15
dopamine 53
dose-response relationship 165
Down Syndrome 94, 95
downplaying positives 84
drugs 2

early puberty 49-51
Edison, Thomas 19

education 15, 25, 27-8, 149
Einstein, Albert 41
electric light bulb 19
electrical power distribution system 19
elephants 5, 6
Ellis, Mark 119
emotionally absent 3
empathic capacity 24, 122
employment 19
ethical framework 47
exaggerating negatives 84
example 34
exercise 27, 28, 86, 92, 101
eye contact 30

father factor 2, 5-8, 14, 16, 19, 21, 130
fatherhood 7-9, 14, 33, 92, 157, 160
fatherless youth 5
fear 43, 102, 147, 150, 153
feedback 37-8, 40
Ferguson, Niall 47
Feuerstein, Reuven 93
Feynman, Melville 41
film camera 19
financial provision 12, 16, 75
First Things First 15
Fischer, Bobby 38
focus (or worship) mechanism 113, 120, 127, 130

forgiveness 24, 59, 63, 70, 71, 73, 75, 78, 87, 91, 92, 99, 115, 118, 123, 129, 155

gate-keeper 131
Gates, Bill 38
genealogy 132
Glueck Study 24
Grandfathers 43
Grant Study 17, 18, 19, 21, 22, 23, 24, 26, 27, 67, 69, 70, 107, 122, 125, 131
gratitude 7, 44, 61, 70, 126
guilt 43, 54, 155

happiness 1, 7, 17, 18, 21, 22, 24, 26, 28, 43, 61, 67, 79, 83, 106, 107, 120, 121, 122, 125, 127, 129, 130, 131, 152
Harvard 17, 22, 47
Hetfield, James 98
Howard, John 92
Hoyt, Rick 31
hyperactivity 10

industrial revolution 58
infant mortality 46
inspirational belief mechanism 113, 114, 127, 130
instrumental variables 171
inter-generational love 18
IQ 18, 93

Jerusalem 93, 94, 95
joke telling 30
Joy, Iris 25

Kennedy, John F. 17
Kruger National Park 5

laughter 30
learning 28, 34, 35, 108, 168
lemons into lemonade 24, 25, 125, 127, 130
life satisfaction 21, 28, 43, 106, 120
life-long learners 27
long-term effects 17, 60
Los Alamos Laboratories 41

Manhattan Project 41
marital instability 11, 16
marriage rates 11, 16
maximum lifetime wage 18-19, 23
McCall, Kenneth 124
McCartney, Jim 40
menALIVE 82
mental health 59, 70, 106, 122, 127
mental illness 20
Merlin Carothers 125
miscarriage 124-5
money 3, 75, 108, 121, 131, 149
mother factor 2, 19, 21, 130
mothers 5, 9, 16, 19, 21, 28-30, 32-3, 46, 55, 61, 92, 101-2, 105

Motivational Enhancement Therapy 169
Mozart, Wolfgang 42
musth 6

nanotechnology 41
narcissistic personality 167
natural burden bearers 123-5
neural pathways 120, 122
neuronal connections 29
New York City 45, 48
Newton, Isaac 107
Nobel Prize 41, 68, 131
nucleus basalis 34
nurture 4, 32, 39-40, 42, 49, 68, 80, 82, 107, 132
nutrition 101

obese 27
obesity 46, 59
occult 122
odds ratio 171
offspring 7
omnipotence 167
Osteen, Joel 35
overgeneralising 84
oxytocin 29-30, 32, 53, 83, 95

package deal 102
Panama Canal 45
parental initiative 89

Pazniewski, Roman 89
peer groups 10, 119
perseverance 27
Pilanesburg National Park 5-6
play 3, 7, 21, 30, 32, 39, 48, 156, 160
poor fathering 5, 7, 16, 52, 65
pornography 52-5, 121
post-partum experiences 46
predictability of effects 165
preferred language of love 64
Project Match 167
propensity scores 171
prospective studies 17
protection 33, 159
psychotherapy 69

quality of life 20, 104, 130
quantum computing 41
questioning 33

randomised controlled trials 165
rebellion 60-1
reflection 3, 37, 40, 54, 71, 93, 158
relationship (or love) factor 2, 18
religious practice 47-8, 51, 106, 127
re-parenting 118
resentment 80, 104
resiliance factor 24
restoration 131
restoration factor 24
retirement 26

risk-taking 38
Roosevelt, Theodore 45, 48
root causes 78

Schneerson, Menachem Mendel 95
school 3, 8-10, 41, 43, 54, 59, 61, 81, 94, 108, 110, 147-9, 157, 158, 160
Seles, Monica 39
self-care 27
self-discipline 38
self-efficacy 168
self-governance 168
setting boundaries 34
sexual intercourse 30
sexually active teens 47
sibling factor 23
singing 30
single parent families 2
smoking 10, 22, 26, 165
social influences 168
socio-economic status 18
sons 5, 8-9, 40, 59-61, 63, 66-7, 89, 99, 119, 162
sound recording device 19
specificity 165
spirituality 7, 106-9, 112, 113, 127, 130, 169
stable marriage 11, 27-8, 102
Stanley, Sheneau 91
step-fathers 50
Stockholm syndrome 93

strength of effect 165
substitute fathers 43, 48, 51, 115
substitute sources 70, 75, 82, 108
success 1, 7, 17-19, 25, 26, 28, 36, 61, 66, 83, 92, 102, 106, 114, 120, 122, 129-30
suicide 11, 69, 116, 121, 132
supportive community mechanism 113

talent 37, 42
teen pregnancy 2, 47, 49, 80-1
teenage syndrome 10
telephone 20-1
Terman Study 24
Tesla, Nikola 22
theme park visits 30
trauma 92-5, 99, 152
TV 58, 59, 65
Twelve Step 28, 54, 62, 73-4, 81, 88, 95, 99, 129, 166
two parent families 2, 14, 47, 80

umbilical cord 31
unwed pregnancies 15

vandalism 11
vasopressin 29-30, 32, 53, 83, 95
violence 11, 56, 59, 65, 111, 147
vocabulary 33
von Neumann, John 41

warmth of relationships 18-19
wealth 20, 22, 121
white rhinoceroses 6
Wilkerson, David 110

work 1, 11, 14, 18-19, 22, 29, 35, 37, 41-2, 45, 48, 58, 65, 77-9, 84, 92, 94, 96, 99, 104, 119, 149, 158, 161, 163-4, 167

About the authors

Peter O'Shea has been working with young people for over 30 years, first as a youth leader and then as a teacher. He has worked as an academic for the past 23 years, during which time he has been employed at the University of Queensland (UQ), the Queensland University of Technology (QUT) and Royal Melbourne Institute of Technology (RMIT). He was appointed as a Professor in the Faculty of Built Environment and Engineering at QUT in 2007, and is currently an Adjunct Professor at QUT. He also worked as a sessional teacher and sessional academic at UQ between 2012 and 2014. His interests are broad and he has published across a range of different areas. He has won various awards for teaching and research, including a Vice-Chancellor's Excellence Award at QUT in 2011, a Vice-Chancellor's Performance Award at QUT in 2010, an Australian Learning and Teaching Council Award in 2007, a Vice-Chancellor's Teaching Award at QUT in 2005, a Best Paper Award at the IEEE Region 10 Conference in 2005, a Faculty Publication award at QUT in 2005 and a Vice Chancellor's Teaching Award at RMIT in 2001. He served as Director of Higher Degree Research in his Faculty at QUT from 2006-2007, and as Director of Teaching Quality Improvement in his School at QUT from 2010-2011.

Robert Falzon is a husband, father, businessman, author and co-founder of *menALIVE*. He has been married to Alicia for 31 years and has 4 children; Isaac (27), Matthias (21), Chiara (18) and Shem (16). He has a degree from the University of Newcastle, NSW, and is a successful business owner. He has been awarded many business accolades including: Australian Marketing Institute - Marketer of the Year, Telstra QLD Small Business of the Year, Australian Institute of Management - Owner Manager of the Year, Ernst and Young Entrepreneur of the

Year Finalist. He has also been a judge in the Telstra Small Business of the Year Regional and National Awards and the Telstra Business Woman of the Year Awards, Regional and National. In 2003 Robert co-founded a men's outreach initiative called *menALIVE*, the purpose of which is to support men and equip them for leadership. In 2007 Robert sold his primary manufacturing business to focus in a full time volunteer capacity on his work with *menALIVE*. Since its founding in 2003, *menALIVE* has delivered approximately 200 events in Australia and NZ for more than 12,500 men. Robert is still involved and owner of a few small private companies: Enviro Framing Systems International p/l, Minnis and Samson p/l and Table and Desk p/l.

www.ingramcontent.com/pod-product-compliance
Ingram Content Group UK Ltd.
Pitfield, Milton Keynes, MK11 3LW, UK
UKHW021956220326
11408UKWH00003B/349